Be
Compassionate

New Testament
BE Books
by Warren Wiersbe

Be Compassionate

AN EXPOSITORY STUDY OF LUKE 1–13

Warren W. Wiersbe

ChariotVICTOR
PUBLISHING
A DIVISION OF COOK COMMUNICATIONS

In this book, Scripture references without book designa-
tions (e.g., 3:2; 7:5; 20:6) always refer to the Gospel of
Luke. All other references include the Bible book desig-
nations (e.g., Acts 3:5; 6:2; John 3:16), but where confusion may result, Luke references also include the Luke
designation. References without chapter designation
(e.g., vv. 2, 6-10) relate to the Luke passage under con-
sideration in the study.

Unless otherwise noted, Scripture quotations are from the
King James Version. Other quotations are from the *New
American Standard Bible* (NASB), © the Lockman Foundation
1960, 1962, 1963, 1968, 1971, 1972, 1973, 1975, 1977; the
Holy Bible, New International Version (NIV), © 1973, 1978,
1984, International Bible Society, used by permission of
Zondervan Bible Publishers; *The New King James Version*
(NKJV), © 1979, 1980, 1982, Thomas Nelson, Inc., Publishers;
the *American Standard Version* (ASV); and *The New Testament: An Expanded Translation* (ET) by Kenneth S. Wuest, ©
1961 by the Wm. B. Eerdmans Publishing Company. Used by
permission.

Cover Design: iDesignEtc.
Cover Photo: Faust Reynolds
Study Questions: Mary Tucker

   10 11 12 13 14 15   Printing/Year   03 02 01 00

Recommended Dewey Decimal Classification: 228
Suggested Subject Headings: BIBLE, N.T.; LUKE

Library of Congress Catalog Card Number: 88-60197
ISBN: 0-89693-591-4

Chariot Victor Publishing,
a division of Cook Communications, Colorado Springs, Colorado 80918
Cook Communications, Paris, Ontario
Kingsway Communications, Eastbourne, England

© 1988 by SP Publications, Inc.

CONTENTS

Dedicated to my friend and physician
DR. DALE E. MICHELS,
who shares with Dr. Luke

a love for Jesus Christ,
a compassionate heart,

and a concern to reach the world
with the Gospel

PREFACE

"Pity is a depressant," wrote the eccentric philosopher Friedrich Nietzche. "A man loses power when he pities."

Nietzche went mad in the year Adolph Hitler was born, but Hitler carried on that philosophy. He despised other people and stood apart from them. He especially despised the weak and the handicapped, and he developed programs for exterminating them.

Robert Payne wrote, "Even on festive occasions he remained singularly alone, the flow of emotion ceasing abruptly when it came in contact with him. . . . He demanded for himself an immunity from people" (*The Life and Death of Adolph Hitler*, Praeger, p. 461).

What a contrast to Jesus Christ, the compassionate Son of Man! In his Gospel, Dr. Luke describes our Lord as one who mingled with people, including publicans and sinners, and who shared the burdens of the afflicted and the weak. Jesus has proved conclusively that pity is a sign of strength, not of weakness; and that God's power flows through loving hearts.

I think it was George Bernard Shaw who said that if the other planets are inhabited, they must be using the earth as their insane asylum. Our world is filled with hurting people who need a loving touch and a word of encouragement. Jesus has put His people here to let the world know that He cares.

His command to us is, "Be compassionate!"

WARREN W. WIERSBE

Suggested Outline of the Gospel of Luke

Central theme: Our Lord's Journeys as the Son of Man
Key Verse: 19:10
Preface: 1:1-4

I. JOURNEY FROM HEAVEN TO EARTH— 1:5–4:13
1. Birth announcements, 1:5-56
2. The babies are born, 1:57–2:20
3. Jesus' childhood and youth, 2:21-52
4. Jesus' baptism and temptation, 3:1–4:13

II. THE JOURNEY THROUGHOUT GALILEE— 4:14–9:17

III. THE JOURNEY TO JERUSALEM—9:18–19:27

IV. THE MINISTRY IN JERUSALEM—19:28–24:53

1

Hear the Good News!

Luke 1

If ever a man wrote a book filled with good news for everybody, Dr. Luke is that man. His key message is, "For the Son of Man is come to seek and to save that which was lost" (19:10). He presents Jesus Christ as the compassionate Son of Man, who came to live among sinners, love them, help them, and die for them.

In this Gospel you meet individuals as well as crowds, women and children as well as men, poor people as well as rich people, and sinners along with saints. It's a book with a message for *everybody*, because Luke's emphasis is on the universality of Jesus Christ and His salvation: "good tidings of great joy, which shall be to all people" (2:10).

Dr. Luke is named only three times in the New Testament, in Colossians 4:14; 2 Timothy 4:11; and Philemon 24. He wrote Acts (compare Luke 1:1-4 with Acts 1:1) and traveled with Paul (note the "we" sections in Acts 16:10-17, 20:4-15, 21:1-18, and 27:1–28:16). He was probably a Gentile (compare Colossians 4:11 and 14) and was trained as a physician. No wonder he began his book with detailed accounts of the births of two important babies! No wonder he emphasized

Christ's sympathy for hurting people! He wrote with the mind of a careful historian and with the heart of a loving physician.

The Gospel of Luke was written for Theophilus ("lover of God"), probably a Roman official who had trusted Christ and now needed to be established in the faith. It's also possible that Theophilus was a seeker after truth who was being taught the Christian message, because the word translated *instructed* in verse 4 gives us our English word *catechumen*, "someone who is being taught the basics of Christianity."

The life and message of Christ were so important that many books had already been written about Him, but not everything in them could be trusted. Luke wrote his Gospel so that his readers might have an accurate and orderly narrative of the life, ministry, and message of Jesus Christ. Luke had carefully researched his material, interviewed eyewitnesses, and listened to those who had ministered the Word. Most important, he had the guidance of the Holy Spirit. The phrase *from the very first* (Gk. *anothen*) can be translated "from above," as it is in John 3:31 and 19:11. It speaks of the inspiration of the Spirit of God upon the message that Luke wrote.

In this first chapter, Luke tells us how God's wonderful news came to different people and how they responded to it. You will discover four different responses.

1. Unbelief (1:5-25)

It was indeed a dark day for the nation of Israel. The people had heard no prophetic Word from God for 400 years, not since Malachi had promised the coming of Elijah (Mal. 4:5-6). The spiritual leaders were shackled by tradition and, in some instances, corruption; and their king, Herod the Great, was a tyrant. He had nine (some say ten) wives, one of whom he had executed for no apparent reason. But no matter how dark the day, God always has His devoted and obedient people.

A faithful priest (vv. 5-7). Zacharias ("Jehovah has remembered") and Elisabeth ("God is my oath") were a godly couple who both belonged to the priestly line. The priests were divided into twenty-four courses (1 Chron. 24), and each priest served in the temple two weeks out of the year. In spite of the godlessness around them, Zacharias and Elisabeth were faithful to obey the Word of God and live blamelessly.

Their only sorrow was that they had no family, and they made this a matter of constant prayer. Little did they know that God would answer their prayers and give them, not a priest, but a prophet! And no ordinary prophet, for their son would be the herald of the coming King!

A fearful priest (vv. 8-17). The priests on duty drew lots to see which ministries they would perform, and Zacharias was chosen to offer incense in the holy place. This was a high honor that was permitted to a priest but once in a lifetime. The incense was offered daily before the morning sacrifice and after the evening sacrifice, about 3 o'clock in the afternoon. It was probably the evening offering that was assigned to Zacharias.

You have probably noticed that God often speaks to His people and calls them while they are busy doing their daily tasks. Both Moses and David were caring for sheep, and Gideon was threshing wheat. Peter and his partners were mending nets when Jesus called them. It is difficult to steer a car when the engine is not running. When we get busy, God starts to direct us.

Luke mentions angels twenty-three times in his Gospel. There are innumerable angels (Rev. 5:11), only two of which are actually named in Scripture: Michael (Dan. 10:13, 21; 12:1; Jude 9; Rev. 12:7) and Gabriel (Dan. 8:16; 9:21; Luke 1:19, 26). When Gabriel appeared by the altar, Zacharias was frightened, for the angel's appearance could have meant divine judgment.

"Fear not" is a repeated statement in the Gospel of Luke (1:13, 30; 2:10; 5:10; 8:50; 12:7, 32). Imagine how excited

Zacharias must have been when he heard that he and Elisabeth were to have a son! "Rejoicing" is another key theme in Luke, mentioned at least nineteen times. Good news brings joy!

Gabriel instructed him to name his son John ("Jehovah is gracious") and to dedicate the boy to God to be a Nazarite all of his life (Num. 6:1-21). He would be filled with the Spirit before birth (v. 41) and would be God's prophet to present His Son to the people of Israel (see John 1:15-34). God would use John's ministry to turn many people back to the Lord, just as Isaiah had promised (Isa. 40:1-5).

A faithless priest (vv. 18-22). You would think that the presence of an angel and the announcement of God's Word would encourage Zacharias' faith, but they did not. Instead of looking to God by faith, the priest looked at himself and his wife and decided that the birth of a son was impossible. He wanted some assurance beyond the plain word of Gabriel, God's messenger, perhaps a sign from God.

This, of course, was unbelief, and unbelief is something God does not accept. Zacharias was really questioning God's ability to fulfill His own Word! Had he forgotten what God did for Abraham and Sarah? (Gen. 18:9-15; Rom. 4:18-25) Did he think that his physical limitations would hinder Almighty God? But before we criticize Zacharias too much, we should examine ourselves and see how strong our own faith is.

Faith is blessed, but unbelief is judged; and Zacharias was struck dumb (and possibly deaf, v. 62) until the Word was fulfilled. "I believed, and therefore have I spoken" (2 Cor. 4:13). Zacharias did not believe; therefore he could not speak. When he left the holy place, he was unable to give the priestly benediction to the people (Num. 6:22-27) or even tell them what he had seen. Indeed, God had given him a very personal "sign" that he would have to live with for the next nine months.

A favored priest (vv. 23-25). Zacharias must have had a difficult time completing his week of ministry, not only because of his handicap, but also because of his excitement. He could hardly wait to return "to the hill country" (v. 39), where he lived, to tell his wife the good news.

God kept His promise and Elisabeth conceived a son in her old age. "There is nothing too hard for the Lord" (Jer. 32:17). Apparently the amazement and curiosity of the people forced her to hide herself even as she praised the Lord for His mercy. Not only was she to have a son, but the birth of her son was evidence that *the Messiah was coming!* These were exciting days indeed!

2. Faith (1:26-38)

In the sixth month of Elisabeth's pregnancy, Gabriel brought a second birth announcement, this time to a young virgin in Nazareth named Mary. At least there was variety in his assignments: an old man, a young woman; a priest, a descendent of David, the king; the temple, a common home; Jerusalem, Nazareth; unbelief, faith.

The people in Judah disdained the Jews in Galilee and claimed they were not "kosher" because of their contacts with the Gentiles there (Matt. 4:15). They especially despised the people from Nazareth (John 1:45-46). But God in His grace chose a girl from Nazareth in Galilee to be the mother of the promised Messiah!

When it comes to Mary, people tend to go to one of two extremes. They either magnify her so much that Jesus takes second place (v. 32), or they ignore her and fail to give her the esteem she deserves (v. 48). Elisabeth, filled with the Spirit, called her "the mother of my Lord" (v. 43); and that is reason enough to honor her.

What do we know about Mary? She was a Jewess of the tribe of Judah, a descendant of David, and a virgin (Isa. 7:14). She was engaged to a carpenter in Nazareth named Joseph

(Matt. 13:55), and apparently both of them were poor (Luke 2:24; Lev. 12:8). Among the Jews at that time, engagement was almost as binding as marriage and could be broken only by divorce. In fact, the man and the woman were called "husband" and "wife" even before the marriage took place (compare Matt. 1:19 and Luke 2:5). Since Jewish girls married young, it is likely that Mary was a teenager when the angel appeared to her.

Mary's surprise (vv. 26-33). When you consider Gabriel's greeting, you can well understand why Mary was perplexed and afraid: "Greetings, you who are highly favored! The Lord is with you!" (The phrase *Blessed art thou among women* is not found here in many Greek manuscripts. You find it in v. 42.) Why would an angel come to greet *her?* In what way was she "highly favored" ("greatly graced") by God? How was God with her?

Mary's response reveals her humility and honesty before God. She certainly never expected to see an angel and receive special favors from heaven. There was nothing unique about her that such things should happen. If she had been different from other Jewish girls, as some theologians claim she was, then she might have said, "Well, it's about time! I've been expecting you!" No, all of this was a surprise to her.

Gabriel then gave her the good news: she would become the mother of the promised Messiah whom she would name *Jesus* ("Jehovah is salvation"; see Matt. 1:21). Note that Gabriel affirmed both the deity and the humanity of Jesus. As Mary's son, He would be human; as Son of the Highest (v. 32), He would be the Son of God (v. 35). "For unto us a child is born [His humanity], unto us a son is given [His deity] . . . " (Isa. 9:6). The emphasis is on the greatness of the Son (cf. 1:15), not the greatness of the mother.

But He would also be a King, inherit David's throne and reign over Israel forever! If we interpret literally what Gabriel said in verses 30-31, then we should also interpret literally what he said in verses 32-33. He was referring to God's covenant with David (2 Sam. 7) and His kingdom promises to the people of Israel (Isa. 9:1-7; 11–12; 61; 66; Jer. 33).

Jesus came to earth to be the Saviour of the world, but He also came to fulfill the promises God made to the Jewish fathers (Rom. 15:14). Today, Jesus is enthroned in heaven (Acts 2:29-36), but it is not on *David's* throne. One day Jesus will return and establish His righteous kingdom on earth, and then these promises will be fulfilled.

Mary's surrender (vv. 34-48). Mary knew *what* would happen, but she did not know *how* it would happen. Her question in verse 34 was not an evidence of unbelief (cf. v. 18); rather, it was an expression of faith. She believed the promise, but she did not understand the performance. How could a virgin give birth to a child?

First, Gabriel explained that this would be a miracle, the work of the Holy Spirit of God. Joseph, her betrothed, would not be the father of the child (Matt. 1:18-25), even though Jesus would be legally identified as the son of Joseph (Luke 3:23; 4:22; John 1:45; 6:42). It's possible that some people thought Mary had been unfaithful to Joseph and that Jesus was "born of fornication" (John 8:41). This was a part of the pain that Mary had to bear all her life (Luke 2:35).

Gabriel was careful to point out that the Baby would be a "holy thing" and would not share the sinful human nature of man. Jesus knew no sin (2 Cor. 5:21), He did no sin (1 Peter 2:22), and He had no sin (1 John 3:5). His body was prepared for Him by the Spirit of God (Heb. 10:5) who "overshadowed" Mary. That word is applied to the presence of God in the holy of holies in the Jewish tabernacle and temple (Ex. 40:35). Mary's womb became a holy of holies for the Son of God!

The angel ended his message by giving Mary a word of encouragement: her aged relative Elisabeth was with child, proving that "with God nothing shall be impossible." God gave a similar word to Abraham when He announced the birth of Isaac (Gen. 18:14). That our God can do anything is the witness of many, including Job (42:2), Jeremiah (32:17), and even our Lord Jesus (Matt. 19:26). I personally like the translation of this verse found in the 1901 *American Standard Version:* "For no word of God shall be void of power." God accomplishes His purposes through the power of His Word (Ps. 33:9).

Mary's believing response was to surrender herself to God as His willing servant. She experienced the grace of God (v. 30) and believed the Word of God, and therefore she could be used by the Spirit to accomplish the will of God. A "handmaid" was the lowest kind of female servant, which shows how much Mary trusted God. She belonged totally to the Lord, body (v. 38), soul (v. 46) and spirit (v. 47). What an example for us to follow! (Rom. 12:1-2)

3. Joy (1:39-56)

Now that Mary knew she was to become a mother, and that her kinswoman Elisabeth would give birth in three months, she wanted to see Elisabeth so they could rejoice together. "Joy" is the major theme of this section as you see three persons rejoicing in the Lord.

First is the joy of Elisabeth (vv. 39-45). As Mary entered the house, Elisabeth heard her greeting, was filled with the Spirit and was told by the Lord why Mary was there. The one word that filled her lips was "blessed." Note that she did not say that Mary was blessed *above* women but *among* women, and certainly this is true. While we don't want to ascribe to Mary that which only belongs to God, neither do we want to minimize her place in the plan of God.

The thing that Elisabeth emphasized was Mary's *faith*: "Blessed is she that believed" (v. 45). We are saved "by grace . . . through faith" (Eph. 2:8-9). Because Mary believed the Word of God, she experienced the power of God.

Second, there was the joy of the unborn son, John (vv. 41

and 44). This was probably the time when he was filled with the Spirit as the angel had promised (v. 15). Even before his birth, John rejoiced in Jesus Christ, just as he did during his earthly ministry (John 3:29-30). As John the Baptist, he would have the great privilege of introducing the Messiah to the Jewish nation.

Third, there was the joy of Mary (vv. 46-56), a joy that compelled her to lift her voice in a hymn of praise. The fullness of the Spirit should lead to joyful praise in our lives (Eph. 5:18-20), and so should the fullness of the Word (Col. 3:16-17). Mary's song contains quotations from and references to the Old Testament Scriptures, especially the Psalms and the song of Hannah in 1 Samuel 2:1-10. Mary hid God's Word in her heart and turned it into a song.

This song is called "The Magnificat" because the Latin version of verse 46 is "Magnificat anima mea Dominum." Her great desire was to magnify the Lord, not herself. She used the phrase *He hath* eight times as she recounted what God had done for three recipients of His blessing.

What God did for Mary (vv. 46-49). To begin with, God had saved her (v. 47), which indicates that Mary was a sinner like all of us and needed to trust the Lord for her eternal salvation. Not only had He saved her, but He had also chosen her to be the mother of the Messiah (v. 48). He had "regarded" her, which means He was mindful of her and looked with favor upon her. No doubt there were others who could have been chosen, but God chose her! The Lord had indeed showered His grace upon her (see 1 Cor. 1:26-28).

Not only was God mindful of her, but He was also mighty for her, working on her behalf (v. 49). Mary would have no problem singing "Great Things He Hath Done!" (See Luke 8:39; 1 Sam. 12:24; 2 Sam. 7:21-23; and Ps. 126:2-3.) Because she believed God and yielded to His will, He performed a miracle in her life and used her to bring the Saviour into the world.

What God did for us (vv. 50-53). In the second stanza of her song, Mary included *all* of God's people who fear Him from generation to generation. We have all received His mercy and experienced His help. Mary named three specific groups to whom God had been merciful: the helpless (v. 51), the humble (v. 52), and the hungry (v. 53).

The common people of that day were almost helpless when it came to justice and civil rights. They were often hungry, downtrodden, and discouraged (Luke 4:16-19), and there was no way for them to "fight the system." A secret society of patriotic Jewish extremists called "the zealots" used violent means to oppose Rome, but their activities made matters only worse.

Mary saw the Lord turning everything upside down: the weak dethrone the mighty, the humble scatter the proud, the nobodies are exalted, the hungry are filled, and the rich end up poor! The grace of God works contrary to the thoughts and ways of this world system (1 Cor. 1:26-28). The church is something like that band of men that gathered around David (1 Sam. 22:2).

What God did for Israel (vv. 54-55). "He shall save His people from their sins" (Matt. 1:21). In spite of Israel's destitute condition, the nation was still God's servant and He would help the people fulfill His purposes. God was on Israel's side! He would remember His mercy and keep His promises (Ps. 98:1-3; also see Gen. 12:1-3; 17:19; 22:18; 26:4; 28:14). Were it not for Israel, Jesus Christ could not have been born into the world.

Mary stayed with Elisabeth until John was born, and then she returned to Nazareth. By then, it was clear that she was pregnant, and no doubt the tongues began to wag. After all, she had been away from home for three months; and why, people were likely asking, had she left in such a hurry? It was then that God gave the good news to Joseph and instructed him what to do (Matt. 1:18-25).

4. Praise (1:57-80)

God's blessing was resting abundantly on Zacharias and Elisabeth. He sent them a baby boy, just as He promised; and they named him "John" just as God had instructed. The Jews looked upon children as a gift from God and a "heritage from the Lord" (Pss. 127:3-5 and 128:1-3), and rightly so, for so they are. Israel would not follow the practices of their pagan neighbors by aborting or abandoning their children. When you consider that 1,500,000 babies are aborted each year in the United States alone, you can see how far we have drifted from the laws of God.

"The greatest forces in the world are not the earthquakes and the thunderbolts," said Dr. E.T. Sullivan. "The greatest forces in the world are babies."

Traditionally, a baby boy would be named after his father or someone else in the family; so the relatives and neighbors were shocked when Elisabeth insisted on the name *John*. Zacharias wrote "His name is John" on a tablet, and that settled it! Immediately God opened the old priest's mouth, and he sang a hymn that gives us four beautiful pictures of what the coming of Jesus Christ to earth really means.

The opening of a prison door (v. 68). The word *redeem* means "to set free by paying a price." It can refer to the releasing of a prisoner or the liberating of a slave. Jesus Christ came to earth to bring "deliverance to the captives" (Luke 4:18), salvation to people in bondage to sin and death. Certainly we are unable to set ourselves free; only Christ could pay the price necessary for our redemption (Eph. 1:7; 1 Peter 1:18-21).

The winning of a battle (vv. 69-75). In Scripture, a horn symbolizes power and victory (1 Kings 22:11; Ps. 89:17, 24). The picture here is that of an army about to be taken captive, but then help arrives and the enemy is defeated. In the previous picture, the captives were set free; but in this picture, the enemy is defeated *so that he cannot capture more prisoners.*

It means total victory for the people of God.

The word *salvation* (vv. 69, 71) carries the meaning of "health and soundness." No matter what the condition of the captives, their Redeemer brings spiritual soundness. When you trust Jesus Christ as Saviour, you are delivered from Satan's power, moved into God's kingdom, redeemed and forgiven (Col. 1:12-14).

Where did the Redeemer come from? He came from the house of David (v. 69), who himself was a great conqueror. God had promised that the Saviour would be a Jew (Gen. 12:1-3), from the tribe of Judah (Gen. 49:10), from the family of David (2 Sam. 7:12-16), born in David's city, Bethlehem (Micah 5:2). Both Mary (1:27) and Joseph (Matt. 1:20) belonged to David's line. The coming of the Redeemer was inherent in the covenants God made with His people (v. 72), and it was promised by the prophets (v. 70).

Note that the results of this victory are sanctity and service (vv. 74-75). He sets us free, not to do our own will, because that would be bondage, but to do His will and enjoy His freedom.

The canceling of a debt (vv. 76-77). "Remission" means "to send away, to dismiss, as a debt." All of us are in debt to God because we have broken His law and failed to live up to His standards (Luke 7:40-50). Furthermore, all of us are spiritually bankrupt, unable to pay our debt. But Jesus came and paid the debt for us (John 1:29; Ps. 103:12).

The dawning of a new day (vv. 78-79). "Dayspring" means "sunrise." The people were sitting in darkness and death, and distress gripped them when Jesus came; but He brought light, life, and peace. It was the dawn of a new day because of the tender mercies of God (see Matt. 4:16).

The old priest had not said anything for nine months, but he certainly compensated for his silence when he sang this song of praise to God! And how joyful he was that his son was chosen by God to prepare the way for the Messiah (Isa.

40:1-3; Mal. 3:1). John was "prophet of the Highest" (v. 76), introducing to Israel "the Son of the Highest" (v. 32) who was conceived in Mary's womb by "the power of the Highest" (v. 35).

Instead of enjoying a comfortable life as a priest, John lived in the wilderness, disciplining himself physically and spiritually, waiting for the day when God would send him out to prepare Israel for the arrival of the Messiah. People like Simeon and Anna (Luke 2:25-38) had been waiting for this day for many years, and soon it would come.

God calls us today to believe His Good News. Those who believe it experience His joy and want to express their praise to Him. It is not enough for us to say that Jesus is *a* Saviour, or even *the* Saviour. With Mary, we must say, "My spirit hath rejoiced in God *my* Saviour" (Luke 1:47, italics mine).

2

The Lord Is Come!

Luke 2

Chapter 2 may well be the most familiar and beloved portion in Luke's Gospel. My wife and I still read the first twenty verses together each Christmas Eve, just as we did when our children were growing up. The story is old, but it is ever new; and God's people never tire of it.

Dr. Luke gives us three glimpses into the early years of the Lord Jesus Christ.

1. The Newborn Baby (2:1-20)

"As weak as a baby!" is a common expression that could not be applied to the Baby Jesus in the manger. While He was as weak as any other baby humanly speaking, He was also the center of power as far as heaven was concerned.

His birth drew Mary and Joseph to Bethlehem (vv. 1-7). Augustus Caesar was ruling, but God was in charge, for He used Caesar's edict to move Mary and Joseph eighty miles from Nazareth to Bethlehem to fulfill His Word. Rome took a census every fourteen years for both military and tax purposes, and each Jewish male had to return to the city of his fathers to record his name, occupation, property, and family.

When Mary said "Be it unto me according to Thy word" (Luke 1:38), it meant that from then on, her life would be a part of the fulfillment of divine prophecy. God had promised that the Saviour would be a human, not an angel (Gen. 3:15; Heb. 2:16), and a Jew, not a Gentile (Gen. 12:1-3; Num. 24:17). He would be from the tribe of Judah (Gen. 49:10) and the family of David (2 Sam. 7:1-17), born of a virgin (Isa. 7:14) in Bethlehem, the city of David (Micah 5:2).

All of this occurred just as the Scriptures said, and Caesar unknowingly played an important part. A.T. Pierson used to say, "History is His story," and President James A. Garfield called history "the unrolled scroll of prophecy." If God's Word controls our lives, then the events of history only help us fulfill the will of God. "I am watching over My word to perform it," promises the Lord (Jer. 1:12, NASB).

Mary and Joseph were already husband and wife but since they did not consummate the marriage until after Jesus was born, she is called his "espoused wife" (Matt. 1:18-25). The journey must have been very trying for her, but she rejoiced in doing the will of God, and she was no doubt glad to get away from the wagging tongues in Nazareth.

Mothers in that day wrapped their infants in long bands of cloth to give the limbs strength and protection. The word translated "manger" (vv. 7, 12, 16) is translated "stall" in 13:15, and can mean either a feeding trough or an enclosure for animals. You see ancient stone troughs even today as you travel in the Holy Land, and it is probable that such a trough cradled the infant Jesus. Many scholars believe that our Lord was born in a cave where animals were sheltered and not in a wooden shed such as you see in modern manger scenes.

"Bethlehem" means "house of bread," the ideal birthplace for the Bread of Life (John 6:35). Its rich historic heritage included the death of Rachel and the birth of Benjamin (Gen. 35:16-20; also see Matt. 2:16-18), the marriage of Ruth, and the exploits of David. It is worth noting that the name *Benja-*

min means "son of my right hand," and the name *David* means "beloved." Both of these names apply to our Lord, for He is the Beloved Son (Luke 3:22) at God's right hand (Ps. 110:1).

His birth drew the angels from heaven (vv. 8-14). How amazed the angels must have been when they saw the Creator born as a creature, the Word coming as a speechless baby. The best commentary on this is 2 Corinthians 8:9, and the best response from our hearts is wonder and worship. "Great is the mystery of godliness: God was manifest in the flesh" (1 Tim. 3:16).

The first announcement of the Messiah's birth was given by an angel to some anonymous shepherds. Why shepherds? Why not to priests or scribes? By visiting the shepherds, the angel revealed the grace of God toward mankind. Shepherds were really outcasts in Israel. Their work not only made them ceremonially unclean, but it kept them away from the temple for weeks at a time so that they could not be made clean. God does not call the rich and mighty; He calls the poor and the lowly (1 Cor. 1:26-29; Luke 1:51-53).

The Messiah came to be both the Good Shepherd (John 10) and the Lamb of God sacrificed for the sins of the world (John 1:29). Perhaps these shepherds were caring for the flocks that would provide sacrifices for the temple services. It was fitting that the good news about God's Shepherd and Lamb be given first to humble shepherds.

Shepherds are not easily fooled. They are practical men of the world who have little to do with fantasy. If they said that they saw angels and went and found the Messiah, then you could believe them. God selected hardworking men to be the first witnesses that His Son had come into the world.

First, one angel appeared (Gabriel?) and gave the glad announcement; and then a chorus of angels joined him and gave an anthem of praise. For the first time in centuries, the glory of God returned to earth. If brave shepherds were afraid at what they saw and heard, then you can be sure it was real!

"Fear not!" is one of the key themes of the Christmas story (1:13, 30, 74; and see Matt. 1:20). Literally the angel said, "I announce to you good news, a great joy which shall be to all the people." He used the word which means "to preach the good news," a word Luke uses often in both his Gospel and in the Book of Acts. We see here Luke's emphasis on a world-wide Gospel: the good news is for everybody, not just the Jews.

What was the good news? Not that God had sent a soldier, or a judge, or a reformer, but that He had sent a Saviour to meet man's greatest need. It was a message of peace to a world that had known much war. The famous "Pax Romana" (Roman Peace) had been in effect since 27 B.C. but the absence of war doesn't guarantee the presence of peace.

The Stoic philosopher Epictetus said, "While the emperor may give peace from war on land and sea, he is unable to give peace from passion, grief, and envy. He cannot give peace of heart for which man yearns more than even for outward peace."

The Jewish word *shalom* (peace) means much more than a truce in the battles of life. It means well-being, health, prosperity, security, soundness, and completeness. It has to do more with character than circumstances. Life was difficult at that time just as it is today. Taxes were high, unemployment was high, morals were slipping lower, and the military state was in control. Roman law, Greek philosophy, and even Jewish religion could not meet the needs of men's hearts. Then, God sent His Son!

The angels praised God at Creation (Job 38:7), and now they praised Him at the beginning of the new creation. The whole purpose of the plan of salvation is "glory to God" (see Eph. 1:6, 12, 14). God's glory had dwelt in the tabernacle (Ex. 40:34) and in the temple (2 Chron. 7:1-3), but had departed because of the nation's sin (1 Sam. 4:21; Ezek. 8:4; 9:3;

10:4, 18; 11:22-23). Now God's glory was returning to earth in the person of His Son (John 1:14). That lowly manger was a holy of holies because Jesus was there!

His birth drew the shepherds from the fields (vv. 15-20). The phrase "even unto Bethlehem" suggests that these men were located some distance away, but they were willing to make the trip in order to see the newborn Messiah. Certainly they arranged for others to care for their flocks while they hastened to Bethlehem. Halford Luccock called this "the first Christmas rush," but it was certainly different from the Christmas rushes we see today!

The verb *found* in verse 16 means "found after a search." The shepherds knew what to look for: a newborn baby wrapped in swaddling clothes and lying in a manger. And they found Him! They worshiped Him and marveled at God's grace and goodness and the miracle He had wrought for them.

These shepherds are good examples for us to imitate today. They received by faith the message God sent them and then responded with immediate obedience. After finding the Baby, they reported the good news to others, "glorifying and praising God." *They took the place of the angels!* (vv. 13-14) Then they humbly returned to their duties, new men going back to the same old job.

For some reason, shepherds were not permitted to testify in court, but God used some humble shepherds to be the first human witnesses that prophecy had been fulfilled and the Messiah had been born. The angels have never experienced the grace of God, so they can't bear witness as we can. Telling others about the Saviour is a solemn obligation as well as a great privilege, and we who are believers must be faithful.

2. The Child (2:21-38)

Dr. Luke now tells us about three important meetings in the temple in Jerusalem: the child Jesus met Moses (vv. 20-24),

Simeon (vv. 25-35), and Anna (vv. 36-38).

Moses (vv. 21-24). Note that the word *law* is used five times in verses 21-40. Though He came to deliver His people from the bondage of the Law, Jesus was "made under the Law" and obeyed its commands (Gal. 4:1-7). He did not come to destroy the Law but to fulfill it (Matt. 5:17-18).

Jesus' parents obeyed the Law first by having the child circumcised when He was eight days old. This was the sign and seal of the covenant that God made with Abraham (Gen. 17), and it was required of every Jewish male who wanted to practice the faith. The Jews were proud to be God's covenant people, and they scornfully called the Gentiles "the uncircumcision" (Eph. 2:11-12). It is unfortunate that circumcision became an empty ritual for many Jews, because it proclaimed an important spiritual truth (Deut. 10:15-20; Rom. 2:28-29).

"His circumcision was His first suffering for us," said the late Donald Grey Barnhouse, a Philadelphia minister and author. It symbolized the work the Saviour did on the cross in dealing with our sin nature (Col. 2:10-11; Phil. 3:1-3; Gal. 6:15). In obedience to the Lord, Mary and Joseph gave Him the name *Jesus,* which means "Jehovah is salvation" (Matt. 1:21).

But circumcision was only the beginning. When the child was forty days old, Mary and Joseph had to come to the temple for the purification rites described in Leviticus 12. They also had to "redeem" the boy since He was Mary's firstborn (Ex. 13:1-12). They had to pay five shekels to redeem the Redeemer who would one day redeem us with His precious blood (1 Peter 1:18-19). Their humble sacrifice would suggest that they were too poor to bring a lamb (2 Cor. 8:9). But He was the Lamb!

Our Lord's relationship to the Law is an important part of His saving ministry. He was made under the Law (Gal. 4:4); and though He rejected man's religious traditions, He obeyed God's Law perfectly (John 8:46). He bore the curse of the Law for us (Gal. 3:13) and set us free from bondage (Gal. 5:1).

Simeon (vv. 25-35). Simeon and Anna, like Zacharias and Elisabeth, were a part of the faithful Jewish remnant that eagerly looked for their Messiah (Mal. 3:16). Because of his readiness and eagerness to die (v. 29), Simeon is usually pictured as a very old man, but nothing in Scripture supports this. Tradition says he was 113 years old, but it is only tradition.

"The consolation of Israel" means the Messianic hope. One of the traditional Jewish prayers is, "May I see the consolation of Israel!" That prayer was answered for Simeon when he saw Jesus Christ in the temple. He was a man who was led by the Spirit of God, taught by the Word of God, and obedient to the will of God; and therefore he was privileged to see the salvation of God. How important it is for people to see God's salvation, Jesus Christ, before they see death.

In verses 29-32 we find Simeon's response to seeing Jesus. This is the fifth and last of the "Christmas songs" in Luke. (Elisabeth, 1:42-45; Mary, 1:46-56; Zacharias, 1:67-79; the angels, 2:13-14). It is first of all a *worship* hymn as he blesses God for keeping His promise and sending the Messiah. He joyfully praises God that he has been privileged to see the Lord's Christ.

But his song is also a *salvation* hymn: "For mine eyes have seen Thy salvation" (v. 30). Now he is ready to die! The word *depart* in the Greek has several meanings, and each of them tells us something about the death of a Christian. It means to release a prisoner, to untie a ship and set sail, to take down a tent (see 2 Cor. 5:1-8), and to unyoke a beast of burden (see Matt. 11:28-30). God's people are not afraid of death because it only frees us from the burdens of this life and leads into the blessings of the next life.

Simeon's song is a *missionary* hymn, which is something unusual for a devout Jew standing in the temple. He sees this great salvation going out to the Gentiles! Jesus has restored the glory to Israel and brought the light to the Gentiles so that all people can be saved (see 2:10). Remember that the compassion of Christ for the whole world is one of Luke's major themes.

Then Simeon stopped praising and started prophesying (vv. 34-35), and in his message used three important images: the stone, the sign, and the sword.

The stone is an important Old Testament image of God (Gen. 49:24; Pss. 18:2; 71:3; Deut. 32:31). Messiah would be a "rejected cornerstone" (Ps. 118:22; Luke 20:17-18; Acts 4:11), and the nation of Israel would stumble over Him (Isa. 8:14; Rom. 9:32). Because of Jesus Christ, many in Israel would fall in conviction and then rise in salvation. (Simeon seems to be speaking about one group, not two.) Even today, God's people Israel stumble over the cross (1 Cor. 1:23) and do not understand that Jesus is their Rock (1 Peter 2:1-6).

The word *sign* means "a miracle," not so much as a demonstration of power but as a revelation of divine truth. Our Lord's miracles in John's Gospel are called "signs" because they reveal special truths about Him (John 20:30-31). Jesus Christ is God's miracle; and yet, instead of admiring Him, the people attacked Him and spoke against Him. His birth was a miracle, yet they slandered it (John 8:41). They said His miracles were done in the power of Satan (Matt. 12:22-24) and that His character was questionable (John 8:48, 52; 9:16, 24). They slandered His death (Ps. 22:6-8; Matt. 27:39-44) and lied about His resurrection (Matt. 27:62-66). Today, people are even speaking against His coming again (2 Peter 3).

But the way people speak about Jesus Christ is evidence of what is in their hearts. He is not only the "salvation stone" and the "judgment stone" (Dan. 2:34, 45), but He is also the "touchstone" that exposes what people are really like. "What think ye of Christ?" (Matt. 22:42) is still the most important question for anybody to answer (1 John 4:1-3).

The image of the sword was for Mary alone, and it spoke of

the suffering and sorrow she would bear as the mother of the Messiah. (This suggests that Joseph was dead when Jesus began His ministry thirty years later, or Joseph would have been included.) The Greek word means a large sword such as Goliath used (1 Sam. 17:51), and the verb means "constantly keep on piercing."

During our Lord's life and ministry, Mary did experience more and more sorrow until one day she stood by His cross and saw Him suffer and die (John 19:25-27). However, without minimizing her devotion, Mary's personal pain must not in any way be made a part of Christ's redemptive work. Only He could die for the sins of the world (1 Tim. 2:5-6).

How much did Mary and Joseph understand of God's great plan for this miracle Child? We don't know, but we do know that Mary stored up all these things and pondered them (2:19, 51). The word means "to put things together"; Mary sought for some pattern that would help her understand God's will. There were times when Mary misunderstood Him (Mark 3:31-35), and this would add to her suffering. The last time you find Mary named in Scripture, she is in the Upper Room, praying with the other believers (Acts 1:14).

Anna (vv. 36-38). Her name means "grace," and she was a godly widow of great age. There are forty-three references to women in Luke's Gospel, and of the twelve widows mentioned in the Bible, Luke has three (2:36-40; 7:11-15; 21:1-4; and note 18:1-8). It isn't difficult to see the heart of a physician in Luke's presentation.

Widows didn't have an easy time in that day; often they were neglected and exploited in spite of the commandment of the Law (Ex. 22:21-22; Deut. 10:17-18; 14:29; Isa. 1:17). Anna devoted herself to "serving God by worship" through fastings and prayers. She moved from the tribe of Asher and remained in the temple, waiting for the appearing of God's promised Messiah (see 1 Tim. 5:3-16).

God's timing is always perfect. Anna came up just as Simeon was praising the Lord for the child Jesus, so she joined in the song! I would like to have heard these elderly people singing in the temple! Their praise was inspired by the Spirit of God, and God accepted it. But Anna did much more than sing, she also spread the good news among the other faithful members of "the remnant" who were waiting for the redemption of Israel. The excitement began to spread as more and more people heard the good news.

Anna was a prophetess, which meant she had a special gift of declaring and interpreting God's message. Other prophetesses in Scripture are Miriam (Ex. 15:20), Deborah (Jud. 4:4), Hulduh (2 Kings 22:14), Noadiah (Neh. 6:14), and the wife of Isaiah (Isa. 8:3). The evangelist Philip had four daughters who were prophetesses (Acts 21:8-9).

3. The Youth (2:39-52)

Having obeyed the Law in everything, Mary and Joseph returned to Nazareth, which would be our Lord's home until He started His official ministry. There were many Jewish men with the name *Jesus* (Joshua), so He would be known as "Jesus of Nazareth" (Acts 2:22); and His followers would be called "Nazarenes" (Acts 24:5; see Matt. 2:23). His enemies used the name scornfully and Pilate even hung it on the cross (Matt. 21:11), but Jesus was not ashamed to use it when He spoke from heaven (Acts 22:8). That which men scorned (John 1:46), Jesus Christ took to heaven and made glorious!

What did Jesus do during the "hidden years" at Nazareth? Dr. Luke reports that the lad developed physically, mentally, socially, and spiritually (vv. 40, 52). In His incarnation, the Son of God set aside the independent use of His own divine attributes and submitted Himself wholly to the Father (Phil. 2:1-11). There are deep mysteries here that no one can fully understand or explain, but we have no problem accepting them by faith.

Jesus did not perform any miracles as a boy, traditions

notwithstanding, because the turning of water into wine was the beginning of His miracles (John 2:1-11). He worked with Joseph in the carpenter shop (Matt. 13:55 and Mark 6:3) and apparently ran the business after Joseph died. Joseph and Mary had other children during those years (Matt. 13:55-56; John 7:1-10), for the "until" of Matthew 1:25 indicates that the couple eventually had normal marital relations.

Luke gives us only one story from our Lord's youthful years. Joseph and Mary were devout Jews who observed Passover in Jerusalem every year. Three times a year the Jewish men were required to go to Jerusalem to worship (Deut. 16:16), but not all of them could afford to do so. If they chose one feast, it was usually the Passover; and they tried to take their family with them, for it was the most important feast on the Jewish calendar.

People traveled to the feasts in caravans, the women and children leading the way and setting the pace, and the men and young men following behind. Relatives and whole villages often traveled together and kept an eye on each other's children. At the age of twelve, Jesus could easily have gone from one group to another and not been missed. Joseph would think Jesus was with Mary and the other children, while Mary would suppose He was with Joseph and the men, or perhaps with one of their relatives.

They had gone a day's journey from Jerusalem when they discovered that Jesus was missing. It took a day to return to the city and another day for them to find Him. During those three days, Joseph and Mary had been "greatly distressed" (v. 48, "sorrowing"). This word is used to describe Paul's concern for lost Israel (Rom. 9:2) as well as the pain of lost souls in Hades (Luke 16:24-25).

It is worth noting that Luke's phrase *Joseph and His mother* (v. 43) suggests the Virgin Birth, while the phrase "Thy father and I" (v. 48) indicates that Joseph was accepted as the legal father of Jesus (see 3:23). To use verse 48 to disprove the

Virgin Birth is stretching a point.

Whether Jesus had spent the entire time in the temple, we don't know. It certainly would have been safe there and the Heavenly Father was watching over Him. We do know that when Joseph and Mary found Him, He was in the midst of the teachers, asking them questions and listening to their answers; and the teachers were amazed at both His questions and His answers.

Mary's loving rebuke brought a respectful but astonished reply from Jesus: "Why is it that you were looking for Me? Did you not know that I had to be in My Father's house?" (v. 49, NASB) It can also be translated "in the things of My Father" (NASB margin), but the idea is the same. Jesus was affirming His divine Sonship and His mission to do the will of the Father.

The word *must* was often on our Lord's lips: "I must preach" (Luke 4:43); "The Son of Man must suffer" (Luke 9:22); the Son of Man "must be lifted up" (John 3:14). Even at the age of twelve, Jesus was moved by a divine compulsion to do the Father's will.

Since Jesus "increased in wisdom" (v. 52), we wonder how much He understood God's divine plan at that time. We must not assume that at the age of twelve He was omniscient. Certainly He grew in His comprehension of those mysteries as He communed with His Father and was taught by the Spirit.

One thing is sure: Joseph and Mary didn't understand! This was a part of the pain from "the sword" that Simeon had promised her (v. 35), and no doubt it happened again and again as the boy matured. Years later, during His ministry, our Lord's family didn't understand Him (Luke 8:19-21; John 7:1-5).

Jesus is a wonderful example for all young people to follow. He grew in a balanced way (v. 52) without neglecting any part of life, and His priority was to do the will of His Father (see Matt. 6:33). He knew how to listen (v. 46) and how to ask the right questions. He learned how to work, and He was obedient to His parents.

The boy Jesus grew up in a large family, in a despised city, nurtured by parents who were probably poor. The Jewish religion was at an all-time low, the Roman government was in control, and society was in a state of fear and change. Yet when Jesus emerged from Nazareth, eighteen years later, the Father was able to say of Him, "Thou art My beloved Son; in Thee I am well pleased" (Luke 3:22).

May the Father be able to say that about us!

3

This Is the Son of God!

Luke 3–4

"If Socrates would enter the room, we should rise and do him honor," said Napoleon Bonaparte. "But if Jesus Christ came into the room, we should fall down on our knees and worship Him."

Dr. Luke would have agreed with the famous French general, for in these two chapters, he makes it clear that Jesus Christ of Nazareth is indeed the Son of God. Notice the witnesses that he presents, all of whom declare that Jesus is God's Son.

1. John the Baptist (3:1-20)

When he came (vv. 1-2). When John the Baptist appeared on the scene, no prophetic voice had been heard in Israel for 400 years. His coming was a part of God's perfect timing, for everything that relates to God's Son is always on schedule (Gal. 4:4; John 2:4 and 13:1). The fifteenth year of Tiberius Caesar was A.D. 28/29.

Luke named seven different men in 3:1-2, including a Roman emperor, a governor, three tetrarchs (rulers over a fourth part of an area), and two Jewish high priests. But God's Word was not sent to any of them! Instead, the message of God came to John the Baptist, a humble Jewish prophet.

How he came (v. 3). Resembling the Prophet Elijah in manner and dress (Luke 1:17; Matt. 3:4; 2 Kings 1:8), John came to the area near the Jordan River, preaching and baptizing. He announced the arrival of the kingdom of heaven (Matt. 3:3) and urged the people to repent. Centuries before, Israel had crossed the Jordan (a national baptism) to claim their Promised Land. Now God summoned them to turn from sin and enter His spiritual kingdom.

Keep in mind that John did much more than preach against sin; he also proclaimed the Gospel. The word *preached* in verse 18 gives us the English word *evangelize*—("to preach the good news"). John introduced Jesus as the Lamb of God (John 1:29) and told people to trust in Him. John was only the best man at the wedding: Jesus was the Bridegroom (John 3:25-30). John rejoiced at the opportunity of introducing people to the Saviour, and then getting out of the way.

A unique feature about John's ministry was baptism (John 1:25-28; Luke 20:1-8). Baptism was nothing new to the people, for the Jews baptized Gentile proselytes. But John baptized *Jews*, and this was unusual. Acts 19:1-5 explains that John's baptism *looked forward* to the coming of the Messiah, while Christian baptism *looks back* to the finished work of Christ.

But there was something even beyond John's baptism, and that was the baptism that the Messiah would administer (v. 16). He would baptize believers with the Holy Spirit, and this began at Pentecost (Acts 1:5; 2:1ff). Today, the moment a sinner trusts Christ, he or she is baptized by the Spirit into the body of Christ (1 Cor. 12:13).

What is the "baptism of fire"? It does not refer to the "tongues of fire" at Pentecost, for tongues over a person's head could hardly be called a "baptism." John's use of the symbol of "fire" in verses 9 and 17 indicates that he is talking about *judgment* and not blessing. In A.D. 70 the nation experienced a baptism of fire when Titus and the Roman armies destroyed Jerusalem and scattered the people. All unbelievers will experience a baptism of judgment in the lake of fire (Rev. 20:11-15).

Why he came (vv. 4-20). The illustrations used in the chapter help us understand the ministry God gave to John.

To begin with, John the Baptist was *a voice* "crying in the wilderness" (v. 4; also see Isa. 40:1-5 and John 1:23). He was like the herald who went before the royal procession to make sure the roads were ready for the king. Spiritually speaking, the nation of Israel was living in a "wilderness" of unbelief, and the roads to spiritual reality were twisted and in disrepair. The corruption of the priesthood (instead of one, there were *two* high priests!) and the legalistic hypocrisy of the scribes and Pharisees had weakened the nation spiritually. The people desperately needed to hear a voice from God, and John was that faithful voice.

It was John's task to prepare the nation for the Messiah and then present the Messiah to them (Luke 1:16-17, 76-77; John 1:6-8, 15-34). He rebuked their sins and announced God's salvation, for without conviction there can be no conversion.

John is also compared to *a farmer* who chops down useless trees (v. 9) and who winnows the grain to separate the wheat from the chaff (v. 17). Like some "religious sinners" today, many of the Jews thought they were destined for heaven simply because they were descendants of Abraham (see John 8:31-34; Rom. 4:12-17; Gal. 3:26-29). John reminded them that God gets to the *root* of things and is not impressed with religious profession that does not produce fruit. In the last judgment, the true believers (wheat) will be gathered by God, while the lost sinners (chaff) will be burned in the fire.

In verse 7, John pictured the self-righteous sinners as snakes that slithered out of the grass because a fire was coming! Jesus compared the Pharisees to vipers (Matt. 23:33) because their self-righteousness and unbelief made them the children of the devil (John 8:44-45; Rev. 20:2). How tragic that the religious leaders refused to obey John's message and submit to his baptism (Luke 20:1-8). They not only failed to enter the kingdom themselves, but their bad example and false teaching kept other people from entering.

John the Baptist was also *a teacher* (v. 12). He not only preached publicly, but he also had a personal ministry to the people, telling them how to practice their new faith (vv. 10-14). He told them not to be selfish but to share their blessings with others (see Acts 2:44-45; 4:32-37).

Even the tax collectors came to John for counsel. These men were despised by their fellow Jews because they worked for the Romans and usually extorted money from the people. Luke emphasized the fact that Jesus was the friend of tax collectors (5:27ff; 15:1-2; 19:1-10). John did not tell them to quit their jobs but to do their work honestly.

Likewise, the soldiers were not condemned for their vocation. Rather, John told them to refrain from using their authority to get personal gain. These were probably Jewish soldiers attached to the temple or to the court of one of the Jewish rulers. It was not likely that Roman soldiers would ask a Jewish prophet for counsel.

John was faithful in his ministry to prepare the hearts of the people and then to present their Messiah to them. He clearly stated that Jesus was "the Lord" (v. 4) and the Son of God (John 1:34). Because John rebuked Herod Antipas for his adulterous marriage to Herodias, he was imprisoned by the king and finally beheaded. However, he had faithfully finished his God-given assignment and prepared the people to meet the Messiah, the Son of God.

2. The Father and the Spirit (3:21-38)
One day, after all the others had been baptized, Jesus presented Himself for baptism at the Jordan; and John at first refused

to comply (Matt. 3:13-15). He knew that Jesus of Nazareth was the perfect Son of God who had no need to repent of sin. Why then was the sinless Son of God baptized?

To begin with, in His baptism He identified with the sinners that He came to save. Also, His baptism was the official start of His ministry (Acts 1:21-22; 10:37-38). He was "about thirty years of age" (v. 23), and the Jewish Levites began their work at age thirty (see Num. 4:3, 35). But our Lord's words tell us the main reason for His baptism: "for in this way it is fitting for Us to fulfill all righteousness" (Matt. 3:15, NASB). In what way? In the way pictured by His baptism in the Jordan. Many Bible scholars agree that New Testament baptism was by immersion, which is a picture of death, burial, and resurrection. *Our Lord's baptism in water was a picture of His work of redemption* (Luke 12:50; Matt. 20:22). It was through His baptism of suffering on the cross that God "fulfilled all righteousness." (The "Us" in Matthew 3:15 does not mean John and Jesus. It means the Father, the Son, and the Spirit.)

When our Lord came up from the water, the Father spoke from heaven and identified Him as the beloved Son of God, and the Spirit visibly came upon Jesus in the form of a dove. Those who deny the Trinity have a difficult time explaining this event.

This is the first of three recorded occasions when the Father spoke from heaven. The second was when Jesus was transfigured (Luke 9:28-36), and the third was during His last week before the cross (John 12:28).

Only Luke mentions that Jesus was praying, and this was only one of many occasions (5:16; 6:12; 9:18; 28-29; 11:1; 23:34, 46). As the perfect Son of Man, Jesus depended on His Father to meet His needs, and that was why He prayed.

Luke interrupted his narrative at this point to give us a genealogy of Jesus. Matthew's genealogy (1:1-17) begins with Abraham and moves forward to Jesus, while Luke's begins with Jesus and moves backward to Adam. Matthew gives us the genealogy of Joseph, the legal foster-father of Jesus, while Luke gives us the genealogy of His mother Mary. Verse 23 can be translated: "When He began His ministry, Jesus was about thirty years old (being supposedly the son of Joseph), the son of Heli [an ancestor of Mary]. . . . " Mary herself would not be mentioned because it was unusual for women to be named in the official genealogies, although Matthew names four of them (1:3, 5, 16).

By putting the genealogy here, Luke reminded his readers that the Son of God was also the Son of Man, born into this world, identified with the needs and problems of mankind. And, since Joseph and Mary were both in David's line, these genealogies prove that Jesus of Nazareth has the legal right to David's throne (Luke 1:32-33).

3. Satan (4:1-13)

Even the enemy must admit that Jesus is the Son of God. "If Thou be the Son of God" (vv. 3, 9) is not a supposition but an affirmation. It means "in view of the fact that You are the Son of God" (ET). In fact, the fact of His deity was the basis for the first of the three temptations. "Since You are the Son of God," Satan argued, "why be hungry? You can change stones into bread!" Satan wanted Jesus to disobey the Father's will by using His divine power for His own purposes.

Why was Jesus tempted? For one thing, it was proof that the Father's approval was deserved (v. 22). Jesus is indeed the "beloved Son" who always does whatever pleases His Father (John 8:29). Also, in His temptation, Jesus exposed the tactics of the enemy and revealed to us how we can overcome when we are tempted. This experience helped prepare our Lord for His present ministry as our sympathetic high priest, and we may come to Him for the help we need to overcome the tempter (Heb. 2:16-18; 4:14-16). The first Adam was tempted in a beautiful garden and failed. The Last Adam was tempted in a dangerous wilderness (Mark 1:13) and succeeded.

We have at our disposal the same spiritual resources that Jesus used when He faced and defeated Satan: prayer (3:22), the Father's love (3:23), the power of the Spirit (4:1), and the Word of God ("It is written"). Plus, we have in heaven the interceding Saviour who has defeated the enemy completely. Satan tempts us to bring out the worst in us, but God can use these difficult experiences to put the best into us. Temptation is Satan's weapon to defeat us, but it can become God's tool to build us (see James 1:1-8, 13-17).

In the first temptation, Satan suggested that there must be something wrong with the Father's love since His "beloved Son" was hungry. In years past Israel hungered in the wilderness, and God sent them bread from heaven; so surely Jesus could use His divine power to feed Himself and save His life. Satan subtly used this same approach on Eve: "God is holding out on you! Why can't you eat of *every* tree in the garden? If He really loved you, He would share everything with you!"

But the test was even more subtle than that, for Satan was asking Jesus to *separate the physical from the spiritual.* In the Christian life, eating is a spiritual activity, and we can use even our daily food to glorify God (1 Cor. 10:31; Rom. 14:20-21). Whenever we label different spheres of our lives "physical," "material," "financial," or "spiritual," we are bound to leave God out of areas where He rightfully belongs. Christ must be first in *everything*, or He is first in nothing (Matt. 6:33). It is better to be hungry in the will of God than satisfied out of the will of God.

When our Lord quoted Deuteronomy 8:3, He put the emphasis on the word *man.* As the eternal Son of God, He had *power* to do anything; but as the humble Son of Man, He had *authority* to do only that which the Father willed. (Note carefully John 5:17, 30; 8:28; 10:17-18; 15:10, 15.) As the Servant, Jesus did not use His divine attributes for selfish purposes (Phil. 2:5-8). Because He was man, He hungered; but He trusted the Father to meet His needs in His own time and His own way.

You and I need bread for the body (Matt. 6:11), but we must not live by physical bread alone. We also need food for the inner person to satisfy our spiritual needs. This food is the Word of God (Jer. 15:16; Ps. 119:103; 1 Peter 2:2). What digestion is to the body, meditation is to the soul. As we read the Word and meditate on it, we receive spiritual health and strength for the inner person, and this enables us to obey the will of God.

We do not know why Luke reversed the second and third temptations, but since he did not claim to record the events in order, he is not contradicting Matthew 4:1-11. The word *then* in Matthew 4:5 indicates that Matthew's order is the correct one. We do seem to have in Luke's order a parallel to 1 John 2:16: the lust of the flesh (stones into bread), the lust of the eyes (the world's kingdoms and glory), and the pride of life (jump from the pinnacle of the temple); but it's doubtful that Luke had this in mind.

The Father had already promised to give the Son all the kingdoms of the world (Ps. 2:7-8), but first the Son had to suffer and die (John 12:23-33; Rev. 5:8-10). The suffering must come first, then the glory (Luke 24:25-27). The adversary offered Jesus these same kingdoms if He would *once* worship him, and this would eliminate the necessity of His going to the cross (note Matt. 16:21-23). Satan has always wanted to take God's place and receive worship (Isa. 14:13-14).

As the prince of this world, Satan has a certain amount of delegated authority from God (John 12:31; 14:30). One day he will share this authority with the Antichrist, the Man of Sin, who will rule the world for a brief time (Rev. 13). Satan's offer to Christ was valid, but his terms were unacceptable; and the Saviour refused.

Again, Jesus quoted God's Word, this time Deuteronomy 6:13. Satan had said nothing about *service*, but Jesus knew that whatever we worship, we will serve. Service to the Lord is true freedom, but service to Satan is terrible bondage. God's pattern is to start with suffering and end with glory (1 Peter 5:10), while Satan's pattern is to start with glory and end with suffering. Satan wants us to sacrifice the eternal for the temporary and take the "easy way."

There are no "shortcuts" in the Christian life, and there is no easy way to spiritual victory and maturity. If the perfect Son of God had to hang on a tree before He could sit on the throne, then His disciples should not expect an easier way of life (see Luke 9:22-26 and Acts 24:22).

Satan questioned the Father's love when he tempted Jesus to turn stones into bread. He questioned His hope when he offered Jesus the world's kingdoms this side of the cross (see Heb. 12:1-3). Satan questioned the Father's faithfulness when he asked Jesus to jump from the temple and prove that the Father would keep His promise (Ps. 91:11-12). Thus, the enemy attacked the three basic virtues of the Christian life—faith, hope, and love.

The pinnacle was probably a high point at the southeast corner of the temple, far above the Kidron Valley. Satan can tempt us even in the Holy City at the highest part of the holy temple! Following the example of Jesus, Satan decided to quote Scripture, and he selected Psalm 91:11-12. Of course, he misquoted the promise and besides he omitted "in all thy ways."

When a child of God is in the will of God, he can claim the Father's protection and care. But if he willfully gets into trouble and expects God to rescue him, then he is tempting God. (For an example of this, see Exodus 17:1-7.) We tempt God when we "force" Him (or dare Him) to act contrary to His Word. It is a dangerous thing to try God's patience, even though He is indeed long-suffering and gracious.

Our Lord's reply was, "on the other hand, it is written" (Matt. 4:7, NASB); and He quoted Deuteronomy 6:16. *Jesus balanced Scripture with Scripture to get the total expression of God's will.* If you isolate verses from their contexts, or passages from the total revelation of Scripture, you can prove almost anything from the Bible. Almost every false cult claims to be based on the teachings of the Bible. When we get our orders from God by picking out verses from here and there in the Bible, we are not living by faith. We are living by chance and tempting the Lord. "For whatever is not of faith is sin" (Rom. 14:23), and "faith comes by hearing, and hearing by the word of God" (Rom. 10:17, NKJV).

Jesus came out of the wilderness a victor, but Satan did not give up. He watched for other opportunities to tempt the Saviour away from the Father's will. "Let us be as watchful after the victory as before the battle," said Andrew Bonar; and he was right.

4. The Scriptures (4:14-30)

The events recorded in John 1:19-4:45 took place at this time, but Matthew, Mark, and Luke did not record them. They moved right into the Lord's ministry in Galilee, and Luke alone reports His visit to His hometown of Nazareth. By now, the news had spread widely about the miracle worker from Nazareth; so His family, friends, and neighbors were anxious to see and hear Him.

It was our Lord's custom to attend public worship, a custom His followers should imitate today (Heb. 10:24-25). He might have argued that the "religious system" was corrupt, or that He didn't need the instruction; but instead, He made His way on the Sabbath to the place of prayer.

A typical synagogue service opened with an invocation for God's blessing and then the recitation of the traditional Hebrew confession of faith (Deut. 6:4-9; 11:13-21). This was followed by prayer and the prescribed readings from the Law and from the Prophets, with the reader paraphrasing the Hebrew Scriptures in Aramaic.

This was followed by a brief sermon given by one of the men of the congregation or perhaps by a visiting rabbi (see Acts 13:14-16). If a priest was present, the service closed with a benediction. Otherwise, one of the laymen prayed and the meeting was dismissed.

Jesus was asked to read the Scripture text and to give the sermon. The passage He read included Isaiah 61:1-2, and He selected it for His "text." The Jewish rabbis interpreted this passage to refer to the Messiah, and the people in the synagogue knew it. You can imagine how shocked they were when Jesus boldly said that it was written about Him and that He had come to usher in the "acceptable year of the Lord."

The reference here is the "Year of Jubliee" described in Leviticus 25. Every seventh year was a "Sabbatical year" for the nation, when the land was allowed to rest; and every fiftieth year (after seven Sabbaticals) was set apart as the "Year of Jubilee." The main purpose of this special year was the balancing of the economic system: slaves were set free and returned to their families, property that was sold reverted to the original owners, and all debts were canceled. The land lay fallow as man and beast rested and rejoiced in the Lord.

Jesus applied all of this to His own ministry, not in a political or economic sense, but in a physical and spiritual sense. He had certainly brought good news of salvation to bankrupt sinners and healing to brokenhearted and rejected people. He had delivered many from blindness and from bondage to demons and disease. Indeed, it was a spiritual "Year of Jubilee" for the nation of Israel!

The problem was that His listeners would not believe in Him. They saw Him only as the son of Mary and Joseph, the boy they had watched grow up in their own city. Furthermore, they wanted Him to perform in Nazareth the same miracles He had done in Capernaum, but He refused. That's the meaning of the phrase, "Physician, heal thyself." Do a miracle!

At first, they admired the way He taught, but it didn't take long for their admiration to turn into antagonism. Why? *Because Jesus began to remind them of God's goodness to the Gentiles!* The Prophet Elijah bypassed all the Jewish widows and helped a Gentile widow in Sidon (1 Kings 17:8-16), and his successor Elisha healed a Gentile leper from Syria (2 Kings 5:1-15). Our Lord's message of grace was a blow to the proud Jewish exclusivism of the congregation, and they would not repent. Imagine this hometown boy saying that Jews had to be saved by grace just like the pagan Gentiles!

The congregation was so angry, they took action to kill Jesus! St. Augustine said, "They love truth when it enlightens them, but hate truth when it accuses them." That applies well to many congregations today, people who want "gracious words" (v. 22) but who don't want to face the truth (see John 1:17).

In spite of the unbelief of the people in Nazareth, the Scriptures declared that Jesus of Nazareth is God's Son, the Messiah sent to fulfill His promises. The people who do not want Him and who reject "the acceptable year of the Lord" will one day face "the day of vengeance of our God" (Isa. 61:2). How significant that Jesus stopped reading at that very place!

5. The Demons (4:31-44)
Jesus left Nazareth and set up His headquarters in Capernaum (Matt. 4:13-16), the home of Peter, Andrew, James, and John. He taught regularly in the synagogue and astonished the people by the authority of His message (see Matt. 7:28-29). He further astonished them by His authority over the demons.

Why would a demonized man attend the synagogue? Did he know Jesus would be there? Our Lord did not want the demons to bear witness to Him, so He told them to be still and He cast them out. Of course, the demons know that Jesus is the Son of God (vv. 34, 41); and knowing this, they tremble (James 2:19).

After the service, Jesus went to Peter's house, and there He healed Peter's mother-in-law. (Dr. Luke noted that she had a "great fever.") At sundown, when the Sabbath had ended and healing was permissible, a host of people brought their sick and afflicted to Peter's house and asked Jesus to help them. Again, He silenced the demons who confessed Him to be the Son of God.

The Lord must have been weary after such a demanding day, and yet He was up early the next morning to pray (Mark 1:35). It was in prayer that He found His strength and power for service, and so must we.

4

The Difference Jesus Makes

Luke 5

Jesus was concerned about individuals. He preached to great crowds, but His message was always to the individual; and He took time to help people personally. His purpose was to transform them and then send them out to share His message of forgiveness with others. Luke describes in this chapter our Lord's meetings with four individuals and the changes they experienced because they trusted Him.

1. Peter: From Failure to Success (5:1-11)

This event is not parallel to the one described in Matthew 4:18-22 and Mark 1:16-20. In those accounts, Peter and Andrew were busy fishing, but in this account they had fished all night and caught nothing and were washing their nets. (If nets are not washed and stretched out to dry, they rot and break.) Jesus had enlisted these four men earlier, and they had traveled with Him in Capernaum and Galilee (Mark 1:21-39), but then they went back to their trade. Now He would call them to a life of full-time discipleship.

It is possible that at least seven of the disciples were fishermen (John 21:1-3). Consider the fact that fishermen generally have the qualities that make for success in serving the Lord. It takes courage and daring, patience and determination to work on the seas; and it also takes a great deal of faith. Fishermen must be willing to work together (they used nets, not hooks) and help one another. They must develop the skills necessary to get the job done quickly and efficiently.

If I had fished all night and caught nothing, I would probably be *selling* my nets, not washing them to get ready to go out again! But true fishermen don't quit. Peter kept on working while Jesus used his ship as a platform from which to address the huge crowd on the shore. "Every pulpit is a fishing boat," said Dr. J. Vernon McGee, "a place to give out the Word of God and attempt to catch fish."

But there was another side to this request: Peter was a "captive audience" as he sat in the ship listening to the Word of God. "So then faith comes by hearing, and hearing by the Word of God" (Rom. 10:17, NKJV). In a short time, Peter would have to exercise faith, and Jesus was preparing him. First He said, "Thrust out a little"; and then, when Peter was ready, He commanded, "Launch out into the deep." If Peter had not obeyed the first seemingly insignificant command, he would never have participated in a miracle.

Peter must have been surprised when Jesus took command of the ship and its crew. After all, Jesus was a carpenter by trade (Mark 6:3), and what do carpenters know about fishing? It was a well-known fact that, in the Sea of Galilee, you caught fish at night in the shallow water, not in the daytime in the deep water. What Jesus asked Peter to do was contrary to all of his training and experience, but Peter obeyed. The key was his faith in the Word of God: "Nevertheless, at Thy word" (v. 5).

The word translated "Master" (v. 5) is used only by Luke and it has a variety of meanings, all of which speak of authority: chief commander, magistrate, governor of a city, and president of a college. Peter was willing to submit to the authority of Jesus, even though he did not understand all that the Lord was doing. And remember, a great crowd was watching from the shore.

How people respond to success is one indication of their true character. Instead of claiming the valuable catch for themselves, Peter and Andrew called their partners to share it. We are not reservoirs, but channels of blessing, to share with others what God has graciously given to us.

2. From Sickness to Health (5:12-16)

Here was a man who *needed to be changed*, for he was a leper. Among the Jews, several skin diseases were classified as leprosy, including our modern Hansen's disease. In spite of modern medical advances, an estimated ten million people around the world have leprosy. One form of leprosy attacks the nerves so that the victim cannot feel pain. Infection easily sets in, and this leads to degeneration of the tissues. The limb becomes deformed and eventually falls off.

It was the task of the Jewish priest to examine people to determine whether they were lepers (Lev. 13). Infected people were isolated and could not return to normal society until declared "cleansed." Leprosy was used by Isaiah as a picture of sin (Isa. 1:4-6), and the detailed instructions in Leviticus 13–14 would suggest that more was involved in the procedure than maintaining public health.

Like sin, leprosy is deeper than the skin (Lev. 13:3) and cannot be helped by mere "surface" measures (see Jer. 6:14). Like sin, leprosy spreads (Lev. 13:7-8); and as it spreads, it defiles (Lev. 13:44-45). Because of his defilement, a leprous person had to be isolated outside the camp (Lev. 13:46), and lost sinners one day will be isolated in hell. People with leprosy were looked upon as "dead" (Num. 12:12), and garments infected with leprosy were fit only for the fire (Lev. 13:52). How important it is for lost sinners to trust Jesus Christ and get rid of their "leprosy"!

This man not only needed to be changed, but *he wanted to be changed.* Lepers were required to keep their distance, but he was so determined that he broke the law and approached the Lord Jesus personally. Throughout his Gospel, Luke makes it clear that Jesus was the friend of the outcast, and they could come to Him for help. The man humbled himself before the Lord and asked for mercy.

By the grace and power of God, this man *was changed!* In fact, Jesus even touched the man, which meant that He became unclean Himself. This is a beautiful picture of what Jesus has done for lost sinners: He became sin for us that we might be made clean (1 Peter 2:24; 2 Cor. 5:21). Jesus is not only willing to save (1 Tim. 2:4; 2 Peter 3:9), but He is also able to save (Heb. 7:25); and He can do it now (2 Cor. 6:2).

Jesus encouraged the man to see the priest and to obey the rules for restoration given in Leviticus 14. The ceremony is a picture of the work of Jesus Christ in His incarnation, His death, and His resurrection. All of this was done over running water, a symbol of the Holy Spirit of God. This sacrifice reminds us that Jesus had to die for us in order to deliver us from our sins.

Jesus instructed the man not to reveal who had healed him, but the cleansed leper became an enthusiastic witness for the Lord. (Jesus commands us to tell everybody, and we keep quiet!) Because of this witness, great multitudes came to Jesus for help, and He graciously ministered to them. But Jesus was not impressed by these great crowds, for He knew that most of the people wanted only His healing power and not His salvation. He often left the crowds and slipped away into a quiet place to pray and seek the Father's help. That's a good example for all of God's servants to follow.

3. From Guilt to Forgiveness (5:17-26)
Jesus returned to Capernaum, possibly to Peter's house, and the crowd gathered to see Him heal and to hear Him teach.

But a new element was added: some of the official religious leaders from Jerusalem were present to investigate what He was doing. They had every right to do this since it was the responsibility of the elders to prevent false prophets from leading the people astray (Deut. 13; 18:15-22). They had interrogated John the Baptist (John 1:19-34) and now they would examine Jesus of Nazareth.

Since this is the first time the scribes and Pharisees are mentioned in Luke's Gospel, it would be good for us to get acquainted with them. The word *Pharisee* comes from a Hebrew word that means "to divide, to separate." The scribes and Pharisees probably developed out of the ministry of Ezra, the priest, who taught the Jewish people to obey the Law of Moses and be separate from the heathen nations around them (Ezra 9–10; Neh. 8–9). The great desire of the scribes and Pharisees was to understand and magnify God's Law and apply it in their daily lives.

However, the movement soon became quite legalistic and its leaders laid so many burdens on the people that it was impossible to "serve the Lord with gladness" (Ps. 100:2). Furthermore, many of the Pharisees were hypocrites and did not practice what they preached (see Matt. 15:1-20 and 23:1-36). In the Sermon on the Mount (Matt. 5–7), Jesus exposed the shallowness of Pharisaical religion. He explained that true righteousness is a matter of the heart and not external religious practices alone.

The scribes and Pharisees picked a good time to attend one of our Lord's meetings, because God's power was present in a special way and Jesus would heal a man with palsy. If leprosy illustrates the corruption and defilement of sin, then palsy is a picture of the paralysis that sin produces in a life. But Jesus would do more than heal the man; He would also forgive his sins and teach the crowd a lesson in forgiveness.

The paralytic was unable to come to Jesus himself, but he was fortunate enough to have four friends who were able to get him to Jesus. These four men are examples of how friends ought to minister to one another and help needy sinners come to the Saviour.

To begin with, they had faith that Jesus would heal him (v. 20); and it is faith that God honors. Their love for the man united them in their efforts so that nothing discouraged them, not even the crowd at the door. (How tragic it is when spectators stand in the way of people who want to meet Jesus. Zaccheus would have this problem. See Luke 19:3.) When they could not get in at the door, they went on the roof, removed the tiling, and lowered the man on his mat right in front of the Lord!

Jesus could have simply healed the man and sent him home, but instead, He used the opportunity to teach a lesson about sin and forgiveness. Certainly it was easier to say to the man, "Your sins be forgiven!" than it was to say, "Rise up and walk!" Why? *Because nobody could prove whether or not his sins really were forgiven!* Jesus took the harder approach and healed the man's body, something everybody in the house could witness.

Was the man's affliction the result of his sin? We do not know, but it is probable (see John 5:1-14). The healing of his body was an outward evidence of the spiritual healing within. Jesus astounded the religious leaders by claiming to have authority both to heal the body and to forgive sins. The people had already acknowledged His authority to teach and to cast out demons (4:32, 36), but now He claimed authority to forgive sins as well. The scribes and Pharisees could not deny the miracle of healing, but they considered His claim to forgive sins nothing less than blasphemy, for only God can forgive sins. For making that kind of statement, Jesus could be stoned, because He was claiming to be God.

In verse 24, we have the first recorded use of the title Son of Man in Luke's Gospel, where it is found twenty-three times. Our Lord's listeners were familiar with this title. It was used of the Prophet Ezekiel over eighty times, and Daniel applied it to the Messiah (7:13, 18). "Son of Man" was our Lord's favorite name for Himself; this title is found at least eighty-two times in the Gospel record. Occasionally He used the title "Son of God" (Matt. 27:43; Luke 22:70; John 5:25; 9:35; 10:36; 11:4), but "Son of Man" was used more. Certainly the Jewish people caught the Messianic character of this title, but it also identified Him with the people He came to save (Luke 19:10). Like Ezekiel, the Old Testament "son of man," Jesus "sat where they sat" (Ezek. 3:15).

The healing was immediate and the people glorified God. But even more than receiving healing, the man experienced forgiveness and the start of a whole new life. Our Lord's miracles not only demonstrated His deity and His compassion for needy people, but they also revealed important spiritual lessons about salvation. They were "object lessons" to teach spiritually blind people what God could do for them if only they would believe in His Son.

4. From the Old to the New (5:27-39)

When Jesus called Levi, He accomplished three things: He saved a lost soul; He added a new disciple to His band; and He created an opportunity to explain His ministry to Levi's friends and to the scribes and Pharisees. This event probably took place shortly after Jesus healed the palsied man, for the "official committee" was still there (v. 17). And it is likely that Jesus at this time gave Levi his new name—"Matthew, the gift of God" (6:15; see also Matt. 9:9).

Matthew sat at the toll booth and levied duty on the merchandise that was brought through. Since the tax rates were not always clear, it was easy for an unscrupulous man to make extra money for himself. But even if a tax collector served honestly, the Jews still despised him for defiling himself by working for the Gentiles. John the Baptist had made it clear that there was nothing innately sinful in collecting taxes

(Luke 3:12-13), and we have no evidence that Matthew was a thief. But to the Jews, Levi was a sinner, and Jesus was suspect for having anything to do with him and his sinner friends.

We wonder how much Matthew knew about Jesus. Our Lord's friendship with Peter and his partners would put Him in touch with the businessmen of Capernaum, and certainly Matthew had heard Jesus preach by the seaside. Matthew instantly obeyed the Lord's call, left everything and followed Jesus. He was so overjoyed at his salvation experience that he invited many of his friends to rejoice with him (see Luke 15:6, 9, 23).

The scribes and Pharisees criticized Jesus because they did not understand either His message or His ministry. Jesus simply did not fit into their traditional religious life. It is unfortunate when leaders resist change and refuse to try to understand the new things that God is doing. In order to help them understand, Jesus gave four illustrations of what He was doing.

The Physician (vv. 31-32). The scribes and Pharisees saw Matthew and his friends as condemned sinners, but Jesus saw them as spiritually sick "patients" who needed the help of a physician. In fact, He had illustrated this when He cleansed the leper and healed the paralytic. Sin is like a disease: it starts in a small and hidden way; it grows secretly; it saps our strength; and if it is not cured, it kills. It is tragic when sickness kills the body, but it is even more tragic when sin condemns the soul to hell.

The scribes and Pharisees were quick to diagnose the needs of others, but they were blind to their own needs, for they were sinners like everyone else. They appeared righteous on the outside but were corrupt within (Matt. 23:25-28). They may not have been "prodigal sons" who were guilty of sins of the flesh, but they were certainly "elder brothers" who were guilty of sins of the spirit (Luke 15:11-32; 2 Cor. 7:1).

As I was writing this chapter, I received a phone call from a woman in Canada who disagreed with my radio ministry and repeatedly condemned "the judgmental fundamentalists." I tried to reason with her from the Word, but she would not accept it. According to her, there was no hell and I had no right to preach about it. As I quoted Scripture to her, she hung up; all I could do was pause to pray for her, and I did it with a heavy heart.

The first step toward healing sin sickness is admitting that we have a need and that we must do something about it. False prophets give a false diagnosis that leads to a false hope (Jer. 6:14); but the servant of God tells the truth about sin, death and hell, and offers the only remedy: faith in Jesus Christ. The religion of the scribes and Pharisees could offer no hope to Matthew's friends, but Jesus could.

What a wonderful Physician Jesus is! He comes to us in love; He calls us; He saves us when we trust Him; *and He "pays the bill."* His diagnosis is always accurate and His cure is perfect and complete. No wonder Matthew was so happy and wanted to share the good news with his friends!

The Bridegroom (vv. 33-35). The scribes and Pharisees were not only upset at the disciples' friends, but also at their obvious joy as they fellowshipped with Jesus and the guests. We get the impression that the Pharisees experienced little if any joy in the practice of their religion (see Matt. 6:16 and Luke 15:25-32). Jesus was "a man of sorrows" (Isa. 53:3), but He was also filled with joy (Luke 10:21; John 15:11 and 17:13).

Jewish weddings lasted a week and were times of great joy and celebration. By using this image, Jesus was saying to His critics, "I came to make life a wedding feast, not a funeral. If you know the Bridegroom, then you can share His joy." He said that one day He would be "taken away," which suggested rejection and death; but meanwhile, there was good reason for joy, for sinners were coming to repentance.

Fasting is found often in the Old Testament, but nowhere is it commanded in the New Testament. However, the example of the prophets and the early church is certainly significant for believers today. Our Lord's words in Matthew 6:16-18 assume that we will fast ("when," not "if"), and passages like Acts 13:1-3 and 14:23 indicate that fasting was a practice of the early church (see also 1 Cor. 7:5; 2 Cor. 6:5; 11:27).

The garment (v. 36). Jesus did not come to patch up the old; He came to give the new. The Pharisees would admit that Judaism was not all it could be, and perhaps they hoped that Jesus would work with them in reviving the old religion. But Jesus showed the foolishness of this approach by contrasting two garments, an old one and a new one. If you take a patch from a new garment and sew it to an old garment, you ruin both of them. The new garment has a hole in it, and the old garment has a patch that does not match and that will tear away when the garment is washed.

In Scripture, garments are sometimes used to picture character and conduct (Col. 3:8-17). Isaiah wrote about a "robe of righteousness" (Isa. 61:10; see also 2 Cor. 5:21), and he warned against our trusting our own good works for salvation (Isa. 64:6). Many people have a "patchwork" religion of their own making, instead of trusting Christ for the robe of salvation that He gives by grace.

The wineskins (vv. 37-39). If unfermented wine is put into brittle old wineskins, the gas will burst the skins and both the skins and the wine will be lost. The new life of the Spirit could not be forced into the old wineskins of Judaism. Jesus was revealing that the ancient Jewish religion was getting old and would soon be replaced (see Heb. 8:13). Most of the Jews preferred the old and refused the new. It was not until A.D. 70, when the Romans destroyed Jerusalem and the temple, and scattered the people, that the Jewish religion *as described in the Law* came to an end. Today, the Jews do not have a priesthood, a temple or an altar; so they cannot practice their religion as their ancestors did (see Hosea 3:4).

The things in the ceremonial law were fulfilled by Jesus Christ, so there is no need today for sacrifices, priests, temples, and ceremonies. All of God's people are priests who bring spiritual sacrifices to the Lord (1 Peter 2:5, 9). The tables of law have been replaced by the tables of the human heart, where God's Spirit is writing the Word and making us like Jesus Christ (2 Cor. 3:1-3, 18).

Jesus Christ still offers "all things new" (Rev. 21:5). As the Physician, He offers sinners new life and spiritual health. As the Bridegroom, He brings new love and joy. He gives us the robe of righteousness and the wine of the Spirit (Eph. 5:18; also see Acts 2:13). Life is a feast, not a famine or a funeral; and Jesus Christ is the only one who can make that kind of a difference in our lives.

5

So What's New? Everything!

Luke 6

For over a year, Jesus ministered as a popular itinerant teacher and healer, and multitudes followed Him. But now the time had come for Him to "organize" His followers and declare just what His kingdom was all about.

In this chapter, we see the Lord Jesus establishing three new spiritual entities to replace that which was now "worn out" in the Jewish religion: a new Sabbath, a new nation, and a new blessing in the new spiritual kingdom.

1. A New Sabbath (6:1-11)

The sanctity of the seventh day was a distinctive part of the Jewish faith. God gave Israel the Sabbath law at Sinai (Neh. 9:13-14) and made it a sign between Him and the nation (Ex. 20:8-11; 31:12-17). The word *Sabbath* means "rest" and is linked with God's cessation of work after the six days of creation (Gen. 2:2-3). Some of the rabbis taught that Messiah could not come until Israel had perfectly kept the Sabbath, so obeying this law was very important both personally and nationally.

To call Sunday "the Sabbath" is to confuse the first day and the seventh day and what each signifies. The Sabbath is a reminder of the completion of "the old creation," while the Lord's Day is a reminder of our Lord's finished work in "the new creation" (2 Cor. 5:21; Eph. 2:10; 4:24). The Sabbath speaks of rest *after* work and relates to the Law, while the Lord's Day speaks of rest *before* work and relates to grace. The Lord's Day commemorates the resurrection of Jesus Christ from the dead as well as the coming of the Holy Spirit and the "birthday" of the church (Acts 2).

The early church met on the first day of the week (Acts 20:7; 1 Cor. 16:1-2). However, some Jewish believers kept the Sabbath, and this sometimes led to division. Paul addressed this problem in Romans 14:1–15:13 where he gave principles to promote both liberty and unity in the church. But Paul always made it clear that *observing special days had nothing to do with salvation* (Gal. 4:1-11; Col. 2:8-17). We are not saved from sin by faith in Christ *plus* keeping the Sabbath. We are saved by faith in Christ alone.

By their strict and oppressive rules, the Pharisees and scribes had turned the Sabbath Day into a burden instead of the blessing God meant it to be, and Jesus challenged both their doctrine and their authority. He had announced a new "year of Jubilee" (4:19), and now He would declare a new Sabbath. He had already healed a lame man on the Sabbath, and the religious leaders had determined to kill Him (John 5:18, also note John 5:16). Now He was to violate their Sabbath laws on two more occasions.

In the field (vv. 1-5). It was lawful for a Jew to eat from a neighbor's vineyard, orchard or field, provided he did not fill a container or use a harvesting implement (Deut. 23:24-25). The disciples were hungry, so they picked the heads of wheat, rubbed them in their hands, and ate them. But in so doing, according to the rabbis, they broke the Sabbath law, because they were harvesting, winnowing, and preparing food!

Always alert for something to criticize, some of the Pharisees asked Jesus why He permitted His disciples to violate the Sabbath laws. This was His second offense, and they were sure they had a case against Him. How tragic that their slavish devotion to religious rules blinded them to the true ministry of the Law as well as the very presence of the Lord who gave them the Law.

Jesus did not argue with them; instead, He took them right to the Word of God (1 Sam. 21:1-6). The "showbread" was comprised of twelve loaves, one for each tribe in Israel; and it stood on the table in the holy place in the tabernacle and then in the temple (Ex. 25:23-30; Lev. 24:5-9). Fresh bread was put on the table each Sabbath, and only the priests were allowed to eat the loaves.

But David and his men ate the loaves, and what Jew would condemn Israel's great king? "He was God's anointed!" they might argue, *but that was exactly what Jesus claimed for Himself (4:18).* Not only was He God's Anointed, but He was also the Lord of the Sabbath! When Jesus made that statement, He was claiming to be Jehovah God, because it was the Lord who established the Sabbath. If Jesus Christ is indeed Lord of the Sabbath, then He is free to do *on* it and *with* it whatever He pleases. The Pharisees did not miss His meaning, you can be sure.

God is more concerned about meeting human needs than He is about protecting religious rules. Better that David and his men receive strength to serve God than that they perish only for the sake of a temporary law. God desires compassion, not sacrifice (Matt. 12:7, quoting Hosea 6:6). The Pharisees, of course, had a different view of the Law (Matt. 23:23).

In the synagogue (vv. 6-11). The Pharisees knew that it was our Lord's practice to be in the synagogue on the Sabbath, so they were there to watch Him and to gather more evidence against Him. Did they know that the handicapped man would also be there? Did they "plant" him there? We do not know, and Jesus probably did not care. His compassionate heart responded to the man's need, and He healed him. Jesus could have waited a few hours until the Sabbath was over, or He could have healed the man in private, but He did it openly and immediately. It was a deliberate violation of the Sabbath traditions.

Our Lord's defense in the field was based on the Old Testament Scriptures, but His defense in the synagogue was based on *the nature of God's Sabbath law.* God gave that law to help people, not to hurt them. "The Sabbath was made for man, and not man for the Sabbath" (Mark 2:27). Every man in the synagogue would rescue a sheep on the Sabbath, so why not rescue a man made in the image of God (Matt. 12:11-12)? The scribes and Pharisees had turned God's gift into a heavy yoke that nobody could bear (Acts 15:10; Gal. 5:1).

This miracle illustrates the power of faith in God's Word. Jesus commanded the man to do the very thing he could not do, and yet *he did it!* "For no word from God shall be void of power" (Luke 1:37, asv). God's commandments are always God's enablements.

The scribes and Pharisees were filled with fury. It certainly did not do them any good to worship God in the synagogue that morning. So angry were they that they even joined forces with the Herodians (the Jews who supported Herod) in a plot to kill Jesus (Mark 3:6). Jesus knew their thoughts (v. 8 and Matt. 12:15); so He merely withdrew to the Sea of Galilee, ministered to the multitudes, and then went up to a mountain alone to pray.

Jesus gives a spiritual "Sabbath rest" that is in the heart all the time (Matt. 11:28-30). Unlike the galling yoke of the Law, the yoke that Jesus gives is "well-fitting," and His "burden is light." When the sinner trusts the Saviour, he has peace with God because his sins are forgiven and he is reconciled to God (Rom. 5:1-11). As the believer yields to Christ in daily experience, he enjoys "the peace of God" in his heart and mind (Phil. 4:6-7).

2. A New Nation (6:12-19)

Jesus spent the whole night in prayer, for He was about to call His twelve apostles from among the many disciples who were following Him. A *disciple* is a learner, an apprentice; while an *apostle* is a chosen messenger sent with a special commission. Jesus had many disciples (see 10:1) but only twelve handpicked apostles.

Why did He pray all night? For one thing, He knew that opposition against Him was growing and would finally result in His crucifixion; so He prayed for strength as He faced the path ahead. Also, He wanted the Father's guidance as He selected His twelve apostles, for the future of the church rested with them. Keep in mind that one of the Twelve would betray Him, *and Jesus knew who he was from the beginning* (John 6:64). Our Lord had real human emotions (Luke 22:41-44; Heb. 5:7-8), and it was through prayer that He made this difficult choice.

The names of the apostles are also given in Matthew 10:1-4, Mark 3:16-19, and Acts 1:13 (minus Judas). In all the lists, Peter is named first and, except in Acts 1:13, Judas is named last. The Judas in Acts 1:13 is Judas the brother [more likely "the son"] of James, who is also called Thaddeus in Mark 3:18. It was not unusual for one man to have two or more names.

Simon received the name *Peter* (stone) when Andrew brought him to Jesus (John 1:40-42). Bartholomew is the same as Nathanael (John 1:45-49). The other Simon in the group was nicknamed "Zelotes," which can mean one of two things. It may mean that he belonged to a group of fanatical Jewish patriots known as "the zealots," whose purpose was to deliver Israel from the tyranny of Rome. They used every means at hand, including terror and assassination, to accomplish their purposes. Or, perhaps the word *Zelotes* translates from the Hebrew word *qanna* which means "jealous for God, zealous for God's honor." (It is transliterated in Matthew 10:4 as "Simon the Canaanite" [*qanna*].) Whether Simon was known for his zeal to honor God, or his membership in a subversive organization, we cannot be sure—possibly both.

Nor are we sure of the origin of the word *Iscariot*. It probably means "man [*ish* in Hebrew] of Kerioth," a town in southern Judah (Josh. 15:25). Some connect it with the Aramaic word *seqar* which means "falsehood." Thus, "Judas the false one." The geographical explanation is probably right.

What an interesting group of men! They illustrate what Paul wrote in 1 Corinthians 1:26-29, and they are an encouragement to us today. After all, if God could use them, can He not use us? Perhaps seven of them were fishermen (see John 21:1-3), one was a tax collector, and the other four are anonymous as far as their vocations are concerned. They were ordinary men; their personalities were different; yet Jesus called them to be with Him, to learn from Him and to go out to represent Him (Mark 3:14).

Why twelve apostles? Because there were twelve tribes in Israel, and Jesus was forming the nucleus for a new nation (see 1 Peter 2:9 and Matt. 21:43). The first Christians were Jews because the Gospel came "to the Jew first" (Rom. 1:16; Acts 13:46). Later, the Gentiles were added to the church through the witness of the scattered Jewish believers (Acts 11:19ff) and the ministry of Paul, apostle to the Gentiles. In the church, there is no difference between Jew and Gentile; we are "all one in Christ Jesus" (Gal. 3:28).

It is significant that after Jesus called His twelve apostles, and before He preached this great sermon, He took time to heal many needy people. This was a demonstration of both His power and His compassion. It was also a reminder to His newly appointed assistants that their job was to share His love and power with a needy world. It is estimated that there were

300 million people in the world in Jesus' day, while there are over 5 billion today, four-fifths of them in the less-developed nations. What a challenge to the church!

3. A New Blessing (6:20-49)

This sermon is probably a shorter version of what we call "The Sermon on the Mount" (Matt. 5–7), although some fine evangelical scholars believe these were two different events and Luke simply omitted the parts of the sermon that would not interest his Gentile readers. If they are the same event, the fact that Matthew locates it on a mountain (Matt. 5:1), while Luke puts it "in the plain" (v. 17), creates no problem. Dr. D.A. Carson points out that the Greek word translated "plain" can mean "a plateau in a mountainous region" (*Exegetical Fallacies,* Baker, p. 43).

Jesus went "into the hill country" with His disciples. After a night of prayer, He came down to a level place, ordained the Twelve, ministered to the sick, and then preached this sermon. It was His description of what it means to have a life of "blessing."

To most Jewish people, the word "blessing" evoked images of a long life, wealth, a large healthy family, a full barn, and defeated enemies. God's covenant with Israel did include such material and physical blessings (Deut. 28; Job 1:1-12; Prov. 3:1-10), for this was how God taught and disciplined them. After all, they were "little children" in the faith, and we teach children by means of rewards and punishments. With the coming of Jesus, Israel's childhood period ended, and the people had to mature in their understanding of God's ways (Gal. 4:1-6).

Jesus was preaching to His disciples as well as to the multitudes (vv. 27, 47), for even the Twelve had to unlearn many things before they could effectively serve Him. Furthermore, they had left everything to follow Jesus (5:11, 28), and no doubt were asking themselves, "What is in store for us?" (See

Matt. 19:27.) The Lord explained in this sermon that the truly blessed life comes not from *getting*, or from *doing*, but from *being*. The emphasis is on Godlike character.

This sermon is not "the Gospel" and nobody goes to heaven by "following the Sermon on the Mount." Dead sinners cannot obey the living God; they must first be born again and receive God's life (John 3:1-7, 36).

Nor is this sermon a "constitution" for the kingdom God will one day establish on earth (Luke 22:30; Matt. 20:21). The Sermon on the Mount applies to life today and describes the kind of godly character we should have as believers in this world. Certainly our Lord describes a life situation quite unlike that of the glorious kingdom, including hunger, tears, persecution, and false teachers.

What Jesus did was to focus on *attitudes:* our attitude toward circumstances (vv. 20-26), people (vv. 27-38), ourselves (vv. 39-45), and God (vv. 46-49). He emphasized four essentials for true happiness: faith in God, love toward others, honesty with ourselves, and obedience toward God.

Circumstances (vv. 20-26). Life was difficult for the people of that day and there was not much hope their circumstances would be improved. Like people today, many of them thought that happiness came from having great possessions, or holding an exalted position, or enjoying the pleasures and popularity that money can buy. Imagine how surprised they were when they heard Jesus describe happiness in terms *just the opposite of what they expected!* They discovered that what they needed most was not a change in circumstances but a change in their relationship to God and in their outlook on life.

Jesus was not teaching that poverty, hunger, persecution, and tears were blessings *in themselves*. If that were true, He would never have done all He did to alleviate the sufferings of others. Rather, Jesus was describing the *inner attitudes* we must have if we are to experience the blessedness of the Christian life. We should certainly do what we can to help others in a material way (1 John 3:16-18; James 2:15-17), but we must remember that no amount of "things" can substitute for a personal relationship with God.

Matthew's account makes this clear: "Blessed are the poor *in spirit. . . .* Blessed are they which do hunger and thirst *after righteousness*" (Matt. 5:3, 6, italics mine). Jesus was not glorifying material poverty; rather, He was calling for that brokenness of heart that confesses spiritual poverty within (Luke 18:9-14; Phil. 3:4-14). The humble person is the only kind the Lord can save (Isa. 57:15; 66:2; 1 Peter 5:6). If you compare "The Beatitudes" with Isaiah 61:1-3 and Luke 4:18, you will see that our Lord's emphasis was on the condition of the heart and not the outward circumstances. Mary expressed this same insight in her song of praise (Luke 1:46-55).

Jesus Himself would experience the persecution described in verse 22, and so would His disciples. How can we rejoice when men attack us? By remembering that it is a privilege to suffer for His sake (Phil. 3:10). When they treat us the way they treated Him, it is evidence that we are starting to live as He lived, and that is a compliment. All of the saints of the ages were treated this way, so we are in good company! Furthermore, God promises a special reward for all those who are faithful to Him; so the best is yet to come!

The four "woes" all share a common truth: you take what you want from life and you pay for it. If you want immediate wealth, fullness, laughter, and popularity, you can get it; but there is a price to pay: *that is all you will get.* Jesus did not say that these things were wrong. He said that *being satisfied with them is its own judgment.*

H.H. Farmer wrote that "to Jesus the terrible thing about having wrong values in life and pursuing wrong things is not that you are doomed to bitter disappointment, but that you are *not;* not that you do not achieve what you want, but that you *do*" (*Things Not Seen*, Nishbet [London], p. 96). When people are satisfied with the lesser things of life, the good instead of the best, then their successes add up only as failures. These people are spiritually bankrupt and do not realize it.

Life is built on character, and character is built on decisions. But decisions are based on values, *and values must be accepted by faith.* Moses made his life-changing decisions on the basis of values that other people thought were foolish (Heb. 11:24-29), but God honored his faith. The Christian enjoys all that God gives him (1 Tim. 6:17) because he lives "with eternity's values in view."

People (vv. 27-38). Jesus assumed that anybody who lived for eternal values would get into trouble with the world's crowd. Christians are the "salt of the earth" and "the light of the world" (Matt. 5:13-16), and sometimes the salt stings and the light exposes sin. Sinners show their hatred by avoiding us or rejecting us (v. 22), insulting us (v. 28), physically abusing us (v. 29), and suing us (v. 30). This is something we must expect (Phil. 1:29; 2 Tim. 3:12).

How should we treat our enemies? We must love them, do them good, and pray for them. Hatred only breeds more hatred, "for man's anger does not bring about the righteous life that God desires" (James 1:20, NIV). This cannot be done in our own strength, but it can be done through the power of the Holy Spirit (Rom. 5:5; Gal. 5:22-23).

We must not look at these admonitions as a series of rules to be obeyed. They describe an attitude of heart that expresses itself positively when others are negative, and generously when others are selfish, all to the glory of God. It is an inner disposition, not a legal duty. We must have wisdom to know when to turn the other cheek and when to claim our rights (John 18:22-23; Acts 16:35-40). Even Christian love must exercise discernment (Phil. 1:9-11).

Two principles stand out: we must treat others as we would want to be treated (v. 31), which assumes we want the very best spiritually for ourselves; and we must imitate our Father in heaven and be merciful (v. 36). The important thing is not that we are vindicated before our enemies but that we become more like God in our character (v. 35). This is the greatest reward anyone can receive, far greater than riches, food, laughter, or popularity (vv. 24-26). Those things will one day vanish, but character will last for eternity. We must believe Matthew 6:33 and practice it in the power of the Spirit.

Verses 37 and 38 remind us that we reap what we sow and in the amount that we sow. If we judge others, we will ourselves be judged. If we forgive, we shall be forgiven, but if we condemn, we shall be condemned (see Matt. 18:21-35). He was not talking about eternal judgment but the way we are treated in this life. If we live to give, God will see to it that we receive; but if we live only to get, God will see to it that we lose. This principle applies not only to our giving of money, but also to the giving of ourselves in ministry to others.

Self (vv. 39-45). The four striking figures in this section teach us some important lessons about ministry. To begin with, as His disciples, we must be sure that we see clearly enough to guide others in their spiritual walk. While there are blind people who have a keen sense of direction, it is not likely any of them will be hired as airplane pilots or wilderness guides. Jesus was referring primarily to the Pharisees who were leading the people astray (Matt. 15:14; 23:16). If we see ourselves as excellent guides, but do not realize our blindness, we will only lead people into the ditch (see Rom. 2:17-22).

Verse 40 reminds us that we cannot lead others where we have not been ourselves, nor can we be all that our Master is. In fact, the more we strive to be like Him, the more we realize how far short we fall. This is a warning against pride, for nothing blinds a person like pride.

Continuing the image of "the eye," Jesus taught that we

must be able to see clearly enough to help our brother see better. It certainly is not wrong to help a brother get a painful speck of dirt out of his eye, *provided we can see what we are doing.* The crowd must have laughed out loud when Jesus described an "eye doctor" with *a plank* in his eye, performing surgery on a patient with *a speck* in his eye!

The emphasis here is on being honest with ourselves and not becoming hypocrites. It is easy to try to help a brother with his faults *just so we can cover up our own sins!* People who are constantly criticizing others are usually guilty of something worse in their own lives.

The illustration of the tree reminds us that fruit is always true to character. An apple tree produces apples, not oranges; and a good person produces good fruit, not evil. Believers do sin, but the witness of their words and works is consistently good to the glory of God. In terms of ministry, servants of God who are faithful will reproduce themselves in people who are in turn true to the Lord (2 Tim. 2:2).

The last image, the treasury, teaches us that what comes out of the lips depends on what is inside the heart. The human heart is like a treasury, and what we speak reveals what is there. A man who apologized for swearing by saying, "It really wasn't in me!" heard a friend say, "It had to be in you or it couldn't have come out of you!"

We must be honest with ourselves and admit the blind spots in our lives, the obstacles that blur our vision, and the areas within that must be corrected. Then we can be used of the Lord to minister to others and not lead them astray.

God (vv. 46-49). Our Lord's emphasis here is on obedience. It is not enough merely to hear His Word and call Him "Lord." We must also obey what He commands us to do. All of us are builders and we must be careful to build wisely. To "build on the rock" simply means to obey what God commands in His Word. To "build on the sand" means to give Christ lip service, but not obey His will. It may look as if we are building a strong house, but if it has no foundation, it cannot last. The storm here is not the last judgment but the tests of life that come to every professing Christian. Not everybody who professes to know the Lord has had a real experience of salvation. They may have been active in church and other religious organizations, but if they are not saved by faith, they have no foundation to their lives. When difficulties come, instead of glorifying the Lord, they desert Him; and their house of testimony collapses.

Nobody can really call Jesus Christ "Lord" except by the Holy Spirit of God (1 Cor. 12:3; Rom. 8:16). If Christ is in our hearts, then our mouths must confess Him to others (Rom. 10:9-10). If we are "rooted and built up in Him" (Col. 2:7), then our fruits will be good and our house will withstand the storms. We may have our faults and failures, but the steady witness of our lives will point to Christ and honor Him.

This is the "new blessing" that Jesus offered His nation and that He offers us today. We can experience the "heavenly happiness" and true blessedness which only He can give. The basis for all of this is personal saving faith in the Lord Jesus Christ, for, as Dr. H.A. Ironside once said, "We cannot live the life until first we possess it."

6

Compassion in Action

Luke 7

Compassion has been defined as "your pain in my heart." What pain our Lord must have felt as He ministered from place to place! In this chapter alone, Jesus is confronted with the miseries of a dying servant, a grieving widow, a perplexed prophet, and a repentant sinner; and He helped them all. If a "hardship committee" had been asked to decide which of these persons was "deserving," we wonder who would have been chosen.

Jesus helped them all, because compassion does not measure: it ministers. Bernard of Clairvaux said, "Justice seeks out only the *merits* of the case, but pity only regards the *need*." It was compassion, not justice, that motivated the Great Physician who came "not to call the righteous, but sinners to repentance" (5:32). Let's meet these four hurting people and see our Lord's responses to their needs.

1. The Servant: His Response to Faith (7:1-10)

In the Gospels and the Book of Acts, Roman centurions are presented as quality men of character, and this one is a sterling example. The Jewish elders had little love for the Romans in general and Roman soldiers in particular, and yet the elders commended this officer to Jesus. He loved the Jewish people in Capernaum and even built them a synagogue. He loved his servant and did not want him to die. This centurion was not a Stoic who insulated himself from the pain of others. He had a heart of concern, even for his lowly servant boy who was dying from a paralyzing disease (Matt. 8:6).

Matthew's condensed report (8:5-13) does not contradict Luke's fuller account. The centurion's friends represented him to Jesus and then represented Jesus to him. When a newscaster reports that the President or the Prime Minister said something to Congress or Parliament, this does not necessarily mean that the message was delivered by them in person. It was probably delivered by one of their official representatives, but the message would be received as from the President or Prime Minister personally.

We are impressed not only with this man's great love, but also his great humility. Imagine a Roman officer telling a poor Jewish rabbi that he was unworthy to have Him enter his house! The Romans were not known for displaying humility, especially before their Jewish subjects.

But the characteristic that most impressed Jesus was the man's faith. Twice in the Gospel record we are told that Jesus marveled. Here in Capernaum, He marveled at the faith of a Gentile; and in Nazareth, He marveled at the unbelief of the Jews (Mark 6:6). The only other person Jesus commended for having "great faith" was a Gentile woman whose daughter He delivered from a demon (Matt. 15:28). It is worth noting that in both of these instances, Jesus healed *at a distance* (see Eph. 2:11-13 and Ps. 107:20).

The centurion's faith certainly was remarkable. After all, he was a Gentile whose background was pagan. He was a Roman soldier, trained to be self-sufficient, and we have no evidence that he had ever heard Jesus preach. Perhaps he heard about Jesus' healing power from the nobleman whose son Jesus had healed, also at a distance (John 4:46-54). His soldiers may also have brought him reports of the miracles Jesus had performed, for the Romans kept close touch with the events in Jewish life.

The important word in verse 8 is "also." (It should be in Matthew 8:9 as well, but the KJV omits it for some reason. The NASB has "too" in both places.) The officer saw a parallel between the way he commanded his soldiers and the way Jesus commanded diseases. Both the centurion and Jesus were under authority, and because they were under authority, they had the right to exercise authority. *All they had to do was say the word and things happened.* What tremendous faith this man exhibited! No wonder Jesus marveled.

If this Roman, with very little spiritual instruction, had that kind of faith in God's Word, how much greater *our* faith ought to be! We have an entire Bible to read and study, as well as nearly 2,000 years of church history to encourage us, and yet we are guilty of "no faith" (Mark 4:40) or "little faith" (Matt. 14:31). Our prayer ought to be, "Lord, increase our faith!" (Luke 17:5)

2. The Widow: Jesus' Response to Despair (7:11-17)

Nain was about twenty-five miles from Capernaum, a good day's journey away, yet Jesus went there even though He was not *requested* to come. Since the Jews buried their dead the same day (Deut. 21:23; Acts 5:5-10), it is likely that Jesus and His disciples arrived at the city gate late in the afternoon of the day the boy died. Four special meetings took place at the city gate that day.

To begin with, *two crowds met.* We can only marvel at the providence of God when we see Jesus meet that funeral procession just as it was heading for the burial ground. He lived on a divine timetable as He obeyed the will of His Father (John 11:9; 13:1). The sympathetic Saviour always gives help when we need it most (Heb. 4:16).

What a contrast between the crowd that was following Jesus and the crowd following the widow and her dead son. Jesus and His disciples were rejoicing in the blessing of the Lord, but the widow and her friends were lamenting the death of her only son. Jesus was heading for the city while the mourners were heading for the cemetery.

Spiritually speaking, each of us is in one of these two crowds. If you have trusted Christ, you are going to the city (Heb. 11:10, 13-16; 12:22). If you are "dead in sin," you are already in the cemetery and under the condemnation of God (Eph. 2:1-3; John 3:36). You need to trust Jesus Christ and be raised from the dead (Eph. 2:4-10; John 5:24).

Two only sons met, one alive but destined to die, the other dead but destined to live. The term *only begotten* as applied to Jesus means "unique," "the only one of its kind." Jesus is not a "son" in the same sense that I am, having been brought into existence by conception and birth. Since Jesus is eternal God, He has always existed. The title *Son of God* declares Christ's divine nature and His relationship to the Father, to whom the Son has willingly subjected Himself from all eternity. All the Persons of the Godhead are equal, but in the "economy" of the Trinity, each has a specific place to fill and task to fulfill.

Two sufferers met. Jesus, "the Man of Sorrows," could easily identify with the widow's heartache. Not only was she in sorrow, but she was now left alone in a society that did not have resources to care for widows. What would happen to her? Jesus felt the pain that sin and death have brought into this world, and He did something about it.

Two enemies met as Jesus faced death, "the last enemy" (1 Cor. 15:26). When you consider the pain and grief that it causes in this world, death is indeed an enemy, and only Jesus Christ can give us victory (see 1 Cor. 15:51-58; Heb. 2:14-15). Jesus had only to speak the word and the boy was raised to life and health.

The boy gave two evidences of life: he sat up and he spoke.

He was lying on an open stretcher, not in a closed coffin; so it was easy for him to sit up. We are not told what he said, but it must have been interesting! What an act of tenderness it was for Jesus to take the boy and give him to his rejoicing mother. The whole scene reminds us of what will happen when the Lord returns, and we are reunited with our loved ones who have gone to glory (1 Thes. 4:13-18).

The response of the people was to glorify God and identify Jesus with the Prophet the Jews had been waiting for (Deut. 18:15; John 1:21; Acts 3:22-23). It did not take long for the report of this miracle to spread. People were even more enthusiastic to see Jesus, and great crowds followed Him (8:4, 19, 42).

3. John the Baptist: His Response to Doubt (7:18-35)

Confusion (vv. 18-20). John had been in prison some months (3:19-20), but he knew what Jesus was doing because his own disciples kept him informed. It must have been difficult for this man, accustomed to a wilderness life, to be confined in a prison. The physical and emotional strain were no doubt great, and the long days of waiting did not make it easier. The Jewish leaders did nothing to intercede for John, and it seemed that even Jesus was doing nothing for him. If He came to set the prisoners free (4:18), then John the Baptist was a candidate!

It is not unusual for great spiritual leaders to have their days of doubt and uncertainty. Moses was ready to quit on one occasion (Num. 11:10-15), and so were Elijah (1 Kings 19) and Jeremiah (20:7-9, 14-18); and even Paul knew the meaning of despair (2 Cor. 1:8-9).

There is a difference between doubt and unbelief. Doubt is a matter of the mind: we cannot understand what God is doing or why He is doing it. Unbelief is a matter of the will: we refuse to believe God's Word and obey what He tells us to do. "Doubt is not always a sign that a man is wrong," said

Oswald Chambers; "it may be a sign that he is thinking." In John's case, his inquiry was not born of willful unbelief, but of doubt nourished by physical and emotional strain.

You and I can look back at the ministry of Christ and understand what He was doing, but John did not have that advantage. John had announced judgment, but Jesus was doing deeds of love and mercy. John had promised that the kingdom was at hand, but there was no evidence of it so far. He had presented Jesus as "the Lamb of God" (John 1:29), so John must have understood something about Jesus' sacrifice; yet how did this sacrifice relate to the promised kingdom for Israel? He was perplexed about God's plan and his place in it. But let's not judge him harshly, for even the prophets were perplexed about some of these things (1 Peter 1:10-12).

Confirmation (vv. 21-23). Jesus did not give the two men a lecture on theology or prophecy. Instead, He invited them to watch as He healed many people of many different afflictions. Certainly these were His credentials as the promised Messiah (Isa. 29:18-19; 35:4-6; 42:1-7). He had not established a political kingdom, but the kingdom of God was there in power.

The Greek word translated "offended" gives us our English word *scandalize*, and it referred originally to the "bait stick" in a trap. John was in danger of being trapped because of his concern about what Jesus was *not* doing. He was stumbling over his Lord and His ministry. Jesus gently told him to have faith, for his Lord knew what He was doing.

There are many people today who criticize the church for not "changing the world" and solving the economic, political and social problems of society. What they forget is that God changes His world by changing individual people. History shows that the church has often led the way in humanitarian service and reform, but the church's main job is to bring lost sinners to the Saviour. Everything else is a by-product of that. Proclaiming the Gospel must always be the church's first priority.

Commendation (vv. 24-30). What we think of ourselves, or what others think of us, is not as important as what God thinks. Jesus waited until the messengers had departed and then He publicly commended John for his ministry. At the same time, He exposed the sinful hearts of those who rejected John's ministry.

John the Baptist was not a *compromiser*, a reed blowing in the wind (note Eph. 4:14); nor was he a popular *celebrity*, enjoying the friendship of great people and the pleasures of wealth. John did not waver or weaken, no matter what people did to him. John was not only a prophet, but he was a prophet whose ministry was prophesied! (See Isa. 40:3 and Mal. 3:1.) The last of the Old Testament prophets, John had the great privilege as God's messenger of introducing the Messiah to Israel.

How is the least person in the kingdom of God greater than John? In position, not in character or ministry. John was the herald of the King, announcing the kingdom; believers today are children of the kingdom and the friends of the King (John 15:15). John's ministry was a turning point in both the nation's history and in God's plan of redemption (Luke 16:16).

Verses 29-30 are the words of Jesus, not an explanation from Luke (see Matt. 21:32). They answer the question some of the people were asking, "If John is such a great prophet, why is he in prison?" The answer is: because of the willful unbelief of the religious leaders. The common people accepted John's message and were baptized by him as proof of their repentance. They "justified God," which means they agreed with what God said about them (Ps. 51:4). But the religious leaders justified themselves (Luke 16:15), not God, and rejected John and his message.

Condemnation (vv. 31-35). Jesus compared that generation to people who were childish, not childlike, and nothing pleased them. He was probably referring to the scribes and Pharisees in particular. John was an individual who declared a stern message of judgment, and they said, "He has a demon!" Jesus mingled with the people and preached a gracious message of salvation, and they said, "He's a glutton, a winebibber, and a friend of publicans and sinners!" They wanted neither the funeral nor the wedding, because nothing pleased them.

People who want to avoid the truth about themselves can always find something in the preacher to criticize. This is one way they "justify themselves." But God's wisdom is not frustrated by the arguments of the "wise and prudent." *It is demonstrated in the changed lives of those who believe.* This is how true wisdom is "justified."

4. A Sinful Woman: His Response to Love (7:36-50)

Jesus not only accepted hospitality from the publicans and sinners but also from the Pharisees. They needed the Word of God too, whether they realized it or not. We trust that Simon's invitation was a sincere one and that he did not have some ulterior motive for having Jesus in his home. If he did, his plan backfired, because he ended up learning more about himself than he cared to know!

The repentant woman (vv. 36-38). It was customary in that day for outsiders to hover around during banquets so they could watch the "important people" and hear the conversation. Since everything was open, they could even enter the banquet hall and speak to a guest. This explains how this woman had access to Jesus. He was not behind locked doors. In that day women were not invited to banquets.

Jewish rabbis did not speak to women in public, nor did they eat with them in public. A woman of this type would not be welcomed in the house of Simon the Pharisee. Her sins are not named, but we get the impression she was a woman of the streets with a bad reputation.

Do not confuse this event with a similar one involving Mary of Bethany (John 12:1-8), and do not identify this woman with Mary Magdalene (Luke 8:2; Mark 16:9) as many continue to do.

The woman admitted she was a sinner and gave evidence that she was a *repentant* sinner. If you check a harmony of the Gospels, you will discover that just before this event, Jesus had given the gracious invitation, "Come unto Me . . . and I will give you rest" (Matt. 11:28-30). Perhaps that was when the woman turned from her sin and trusted the Saviour. Her tears, her humble attitude, and her expensive gift all spoke of a changed heart.

The critical host (vv. 39-43). Simon was embarrassed, both for himself and for his guests. People had been saying that Jesus was a great prophet (v. 16), but He certainly was not exhibiting much prophetic discernment if He allowed a sinful woman to anoint His feet! He must be a fraud.

Simon's real problem was *blindness*: he could not see himself, the woman, or the Lord Jesus. It was easy for him to say "*She* is a sinner!" but impossible for him to say "I am also a sinner!" (See Luke 18:9-14.) Jesus proved that He was indeed a prophet by reading Simon's thoughts and revealing his needs.

The parable does not deal with the *amount* of sin in a person's life but the *awareness* of that sin in his heart. How much sin must a person commit to be a sinner? Simon and the woman were both sinners. Simon was guilty of sins of the spirit, especially pride, while the woman was guilty of sins of the flesh (see 2 Cor. 7:1). Her sins were known, while Simon's sins were hidden to everyone except God. *And both of them were bankrupt and could not pay their debt to God.* Simon was just as spiritually bankrupt as the woman, only he did not realize it.

Forgiveness is a gift of God's grace; the debt was paid in full by Jesus Christ (Eph. 1:7; 1 Peter 1:18-19). The word *frankly* means "graciously and freely." The woman accepted God's free offer of salvation and expressed her love openly.

Simon rejected that offer and remained unforgiven. He was not only blind to himself, but he was blind to the woman and to his honored guest!

The forgiving Saviour (vv. 44-50). The woman was guilty of sins of commission, but Simon was guilty of sins of omission. He had not been a gracious host to the Lord Jesus. (For a contrast, see Abraham in Genesis 18:1-8.) Everything that Simon neglected to do, the woman did—and she did it better!

There are two errors we must avoid as we interpret our Lord's words. First, we must not conclude that this woman was saved by her tears and her gift. Jesus made it clear that it was *her faith* alone that saved her (v. 50), for no amount of good works can pay for salvation (Titus 3:4-7).

Nor should we think that lost sinners are saved by love, either God's love for them or their love for God. God loves the whole world (John 3:16), yet the whole world is not saved. "For by grace you have been saved through faith, and that not of yourselves; it is the gift of God, not of works, lest anyone should boast" (Eph. 2:8-9, NKJV). Grace is love that pays a price, and that price was the death of the Son of God on the cross.

Jesus did not reject either the woman's tears or her gift of ointment, because her works were the evidence of her faith. "Faith without works is dead" (James 2:20; also see 2:14-26). We are not saved by faith plus works; we are saved by a faith that leads to works. This anonymous woman illustrates the truth of Galatians 5:6, "The only thing that counts is faith expressing itself through love" (NIV).

How did the woman know that her sins were forgiven? *Jesus told her.* How do we know today that we have been forgiven? *God tells us so in His Word.* Here are just a few verses to consider: Isaiah 1:18; 43:25-26; 55:6-7; Acts 13:38-39; Romans 4:7-8; Ephesians 4:32; and Hebrews 8:12. Once you understand the meaning of God's grace you have no trouble receiving His free and full forgiveness and rejoicing in it.

Of course, the legalistic critics at the dinner were shocked when Jesus said, "Her sins, which are many, are forgiven." By saying this, Jesus was claiming to be God! (See Luke 5:21.) But He *is* God, and He died for the sins that she committed. His words of forgiveness were not cheap words; they cost Him dearly on the cross.

How was this woman saved? She repented of her sins and put her faith in Jesus Christ. How did she know she was truly forgiven? She had the assurance of His word. What was the proof of her salvation? Her love for Christ expressed in sacrificial devotion to Him. For the first time in her life, she had peace with God (v. 50). Literally it reads, "Go *into* peace," for she had moved out of the sphere of enmity toward God and was now enjoying peace with God (Rom. 8:7-8; 5:1).

When Jesus healed the centurion's servant, it was a great miracle. An even greater miracle was His raising the widow's son from the dead. But in this chapter, the greatest miracle of all was His saving this woman from her sins and making her a new person. The miracle of salvation has to be the greatest miracle of all, for it meets the greatest need, brings the greatest results (and they last forever), and cost the greatest price.

Simon was blind to the woman and blind to himself. He saw her past, but Jesus saw her future. I wonder how many rejected sinners have found salvation through the testimony of this woman in Luke's Gospel. She encourages us to believe that Jesus can take any sinner and make him or her into a child of God.

But God's forgiveness is not automatic; we can reject His grace if we will. In 1830, a man named George Wilson was arrested for mail theft, the penalty for which was hanging. After a time, President Andrew Jackson gave Wilson a pardon *but he refused to accept it!* The authorities were puzzled: should Wilson be freed or hanged?

They consulted Chief Justice John Marshall, who handed down this decision: "A pardon is a slip of paper, the value of which is determined by the acceptance of the person to be pardoned. If it is refused, it is no pardon. George Wilson must be hanged."

If you have never accepted God's pardon, now is the time to believe and be saved.

7

Lessons about Faith

Luke 8

One of the major themes in chapter 8 is how to get faith and use it in the everyday experiences of life. In the first section, Jesus laid the foundation by teaching His disciples that faith comes through receiving the Word of God into an understanding heart. In the second part, He put them through a series of "examinations" to see how much they had really learned. Most of us enjoy Bible study, but we wish we could avoid the examinations that often follow the lessons! However, it is in the tests of life that faith really grows and we get closer to Christ.

The cynical American editor H.L. Mencken defined faith as "an illogical belief in the occurrence of the impossible," and Mark Twain said (through one of his characters) that faith is "believin' what you know ain't so." Of course, these men are describing superstition, not faith; for the faith of a Christian rests on solid foundations.

Everybody lives by faith in something or someone. The difference between the Christian believer and the unsaved person is not that one has faith and the other does not. They *both* have faith. The difference is in *the object of their faith,* for faith is only as good as the object. The Christian believer has put his faith in Jesus Christ, and he bases that faith on the Word of God.

1. Teaching: Hearing God's Word (8:1-21)

The Lord continued His itinerant ministry in Galilee, assisted by His disciples and partially supported by some godly women. It was not unusual for Jewish rabbis to receive gifts from grateful people, and these women had certainly benefited from Jesus' ministry. The New Testament church leaders were supported by gifts from friends (2 Tim. 1:16-18) and from churches (Phil. 4:15-17), and Paul supported himself by his own labor (2 Thes. 3:6-10).

The word *hear* is used nine times in this section. It means much more than simply listening to words. "Hearing" means listening with spiritual understanding and receptivity. "So then faith comes by hearing, and hearing by the word of God" (Rom. 10:17). With this in mind, we can understand the three admonitions Jesus gave His followers.

Hear and receive the Word (vv. 4-15). Initially, the sower is Jesus Christ, but the sower represents any of God's people who share the Word of God (John 4:35-38). The seed is the Word of God, for, like seed, the Word has life and power (Heb. 4:12) and can produce spiritual fruit (Gal. 5:22-23). But the seed can do nothing until it is planted (John 12:24). When a person hears and understands the Word, then the seed is planted in the heart. What happens after that depends on the nature of the soil.

Jesus called this parable "The Parable of the Sower" (Matt. 13:18), but it could also be called "The Parable of the Soils." The seed without the soil is fruitless, and the soil without the seed is almost useless. The human heart is like soil: if it is prepared properly, it can receive the seed of the Word of God and produce a fruitful harvest.

Jesus described four different kinds of hearts, three of

which did not produce any fruit. The proof of salvation is *fruit* and not merely hearing the Word or making a profession of faith in Christ. Jesus had already made that clear in His "Sermon on the Mount" (Luke 6:43-49; also note Matt. 7:20).

The hard soil (vv. 5, 12) represents the person who hears the Word but immediately allows the devil to snatch the seed away. How did the heart become hard? The "wayside" was the path that ran through the common field, separating the plots; and the foot traffic hardened the soil. Whatever goes into the ear or eye finally enters the heart, so be careful who is allowed to "walk on your heart."

The shallow soil (vv. 6, 13) illustrates the emotional hearer who quickly responds to the message, but his interest wanes and he does not continue (see John 8:31-32). In many parts of the Holy Land you find a substratum of limestone covered with a thin layer of soil. The shoot can grow up, but the roots cannot go down, and the sun withers the rootless plant. The sun represents the testing that comes to all professing believers to prove their faith. Sun is good for plants *if they have roots*. Persecution can deepen the roots of a true Christian, but it only exposes the shallowness of the false Christian.

The crowded soil (vv. 7, 14) illustrates the person who does not repent and "weed out" the things that hinder the harvest. There is enough soil so the roots can go down, but not enough room for the plant to grow up and produce fruit. The plant is crowded out and the fruit is choked. "Cares, riches and, the pleasures of this life" are like weeds in a garden that keep the soil from being fruitful. The person with the "crowded heart" comes closest to salvation, but he still does not bring forth "fruit to perfection."

The good soil (vv. 8, 15) alone is fruitful. It illustrates the individual who hears the Word, understands it, receives it within and is truly saved, and proves it by patiently producing fruit (see 1 Thes. 2:13; 1 Peter 1:22-25). Not everybody produces the same amount of fruit (Matt. 13:8), but all true believers will produce some fruit as evidence of spiritual life. That fruit may include winning others to Christ (Rom. 1:13), money given to God's work (Rom. 15:25-28), good works (Col. 1:10), Christian character (Gal. 5:22-23), and praise to the Lord (Heb. 13:15).

This parable shows that Jesus was not impressed by the great crowds that followed Him. He knew that most of the people did not really "hear" the Word and receive it in their hearts. He gave this story to encourage the disciples in their future ministry, and to encourage us today. When you consider how much teaching, preaching, and witnessing goes on in the course of a month or a year, you wonder why there is such a small harvest. The fault does not lie with the sower or the seed. The problem is with the soil. The human heart will not submit to God, repent, and receive the Word and be saved.

"Faith comes first to the hearing ear, not to the cogitating mind," said A.W. Tozer, the much-quoted pastor and author. Faith is not a matter of IQ or education; it is a matter of humbly preparing the heart to receive God's truth (James 1:19-21). The wise and prudent are blind to truths that are easy for the babes to understand (Matt. 11:20-26).

Hear and share the Word (vv. 16-18). The disciples were perplexed because Jesus taught in parables, so they asked Him for an explanation (vv. 9-10; also see Matt. 13:10-17). His reply seems to suggest that He used parables in order to *hide* the truth from the crowds, but just the opposite is true, and verses 16-18 make that clear. His teaching is a light that must be allowed to shine so that sinners may be saved.

The word *parable* means "to cast alongside." A parable is a story that teaches something new by putting the truth alongside something familiar. The people knew about seeds and soil, so the Parable of the Sower interested them. Those who were indifferent or proud would shrug it off. Our Lord's parables attracted the attention of the careless and indifferent, and aroused the interest of the concerned.

A parable starts off as a *picture* that is familiar to the listeners. But as you carefully consider the picture, it becomes a *mirror* in which you see yourself, and many people do not like to see themselves. This explains why some of our Lord's listeners became angry when they heard His parables, and even tried to kill Him. But if we see ourselves as needy sinners and ask for help, then the mirror becomes a *window* through which we see God and His grace. To understand a parable and benefit from it demands honesty and humility on our part, and many of our Lord's hearers lacked both.

It is a serious thing to hear and understand the Word of God, because this puts upon us the obligation to share that Word with others. Everyone who receives the seed then becomes a sower, a light-bearer, and a transmitter of God's truth (see 1 Thes. 1:5-8). If we keep it to ourselves, we will lose it; but if we share it, we will receive more.

Hear and obey the Word (vv. 19-21). Our Lord's mother, Mary, and His half brothers (Matt. 13:55-56; Acts 1:14) were worried about Jesus and wanted to talk with Him. Some of His friends had already said that He was out of His mind (Mark 3:21), and perhaps His family agreed with them. Jesus took this as an opportunity to teach another spiritual lesson: being a part of His spiritual family is much more important than any human relationship and is based on obedience to the Word of God. It is not enough to "hear" the Word of God; we must also "keep it" (v. 15).

In one of my radio series, I emphasized the importance of *doing* the Word of God, putting it into practice in daily life (James 1:22-25). I warned listeners that it is easy to think we are "spiritual" because we listen to one preacher after another, take notes, mark our Bibles, *but never really practice what we learn.* We are only fooling ourselves.

A listener wrote that my words had made her angry, but then she faced up to the fact that she was indeed guilty of being an "auditor" and not a doer of the Word. She began to listen to fewer radio preachers, to listen more carefully, and to practice what she heard. "This new approach to Bible study has transformed me!" she wrote. "The Bible has become a new book to me and my life has changed!"

As His disciples, we must take heed *what we hear* (Mark 4:24) and *how we hear* (v. 18), because God will hold us accountable. Listening to the wrong things, or listening to the right things with the wrong attitude, will rob us of truth and blessing. If we are faithful to receive the Word and share it, God will give us more; but if we fail to let our light shine, we will lose what we have. It is a solemn thing to hear the Word of God.

2. Testing: Heeding God's Word (8:22-56)

By the time the Lord had finished giving "The Parables of the Kingdom" (Matt. 13:1-52), the disciples must have felt like postgraduate students in the School of Faith! They now understood mysteries that were hidden from the scribes and rabbis and even from the Old Testament prophets. What they did not realize (and we are so like them!) is that *faith must be tested before it can be trusted.* It is one thing to learn a new spiritual truth, but quite something else to practice that truth in the everyday experiences of life.

Satan does not care how much Bible truth we learn so long as we do not live it. Truth that is only in the head is purely academic and never will get into the heart until it is practiced by the will. "Doing the will of God from the heart" is what God wants from His children (Eph. 6:6). Satan knows that academic truth is not dangerous, but *active* truth is.

Watch the Lord Jesus Christ as He meets four challenges to faith and comes forth the Victor. His people face these same challenges today and can also overcome by faith.

Dangerous circumstances (vv. 22-25). Jesus was weary from a long day of teaching and went to sleep as the ship left

Capernaum for the opposite shore. But before He did, He gave them a word of command that was also a word of promise: they were going to the opposite shore. This word should have encouraged and strengthened the disciples during the storm, but their faith was still small (Matt. 8:26).

While our tour group was sailing from Tiberias to Capernaum, I asked our guide if he had even been in a storm on the Sea of Galilee. His eyes opened wide and he said, "Yes, and I hope it never happens to me again!" The situation is such that sudden squalls occur as winds from the mountains funnel to the lake located 600 feet below sea level. When the cold air and warm air meet in this natural basin, a storm is sure to develop.

The disciples were afraid, *but Jesus was not!* He kept on sleeping, confident that His Father was completely in control (Ps. 89:8-9). The disciples became so frightened that they awakened Him and begged Him to rescue them. The title *Master* is the same one Peter used in Luke 5:5. Of course, their problem was not the storm around them but the unbelief within them. Actually, their unbelief was more dangerous than the storm!

The word *rebuked* was used by Jesus when dealing with demons (Luke 4:35, 41; 9:42). It is possible that Satan was behind this severe storm, attempting to destroy Jesus or at least hinder Him from reaching the demonized men at Gadara. But Jesus calmed both the wind and the sea by simply speaking the word. Usually after the winds die down, the waves remain rough for hours; but in this instance, everything became calm immediately and stayed that way (Ps. 148:8).

The disciples failed this test of faith because they did not lay hold of His word that He was going to the other side. It has well been said that faith is not believing in spite of circumstances; it is obeying in spite of feelings and consequences. The disciples looked around and saw danger, and looked within and saw fear; but they failed to look up by faith and see God. Faith and fear cannot dwell together in the same heart.

A woman said to D.L. Moody, "I have found a wonderful promise!" and she quoted Psalm 56:3, "What time I am afraid, I will trust in Thee."

"Let me give you a better one," said Moody; and he quoted Isaiah 12:2, "Behold God is my salvation; I will trust and not be afraid."

Satan (vv. 26-39). Two demonized men met Jesus when He landed at Gadara (Matt. 8:28), but one of them was the more forward and did all the speaking. Both were pitiful cases: naked, living in the tombs, violent, dangerous, a menace to the area, and controlled by a legion of demons. (A Roman legion could have as many as 6,000 men!) Satan is the thief (John 10:10) who robs his people of everything good and then tries to destroy them. No amount of man-made authority or restraint can control or change the devil's servants. Their only hope is in the Saviour.

Demons have faith (James 2:19), but it is not saving faith. They believe that Jesus Christ is the Son of God with authority to command them. They believe in a future judgment (Matt. 8:29) and in the existence of a place of torment to which Jesus could send them ("the abyss" v. 31). They also believe in prayer, for the demons begged Jesus not to send them to the abyss. They asked to be sent into the pigs, and Jesus granted their request.

Did Jesus have the right to permit the legion of demons to destroy a herd of 2,000 swine and perhaps put the owners out of business? God owns everything (see Ps. 50:10-11) and can dispose of it as He pleases. Furthermore, these two men were worth far more than many pigs (see Matt. 12:12). The community should have thanked Jesus for ridding their neighborhood of these two menaces, but instead, *they begged Him to leave!*

What a transformation in these two men! You would have expected the people who saw the miracle to ask Jesus to stay and heal others who were sick and afflicted. Apparently money was more important to them than mercy, and they asked Jesus to leave.

The one former demoniac kept pleading with Jesus to be allowed to travel with Him and help Him. What a noble desire from a newly converted man! He had more spiritual discernment than all the other citizens put together. The man was not yet ready to become a disciple, but he could serve Jesus as a witness, starting at home among his Gentile relatives and friends. Jesus did not want Jews who had been healed to say too much about it, but it was safe for the Gentiles to tell others what Jesus had done for them, and that is what he did.

Sickness (vv. 40-48). When Jesus returned to Capernaum, the people welcomed Him, particularly a man and a woman who each had heavy burdens to share with Jesus. The contrast here is interesting, for it shows the variety of people who came to Jesus for help. The man's name is given (Jairus) but the woman is anonymous. Jairus was a wealthy leading citizen, but the woman was a lowly person who had spent all her money trying to get well. Here was a man interceding for his child and a woman hoping to get help for herself, and both came to the feet of Jesus. Jairus had been blessed with twelve years of joy with his daughter, and now might lose her, while the woman had experienced twelve years of misery because of her affliction, and now she was hoping to get well.

This woman had a hidden need, a burden she had lived with for twelve long years. It affected her physically and made life difficult. But it also affected her spiritually, because the hemorrhage made her ceremonially defiled and unable to participate in the religious life of the nation (Lev. 15:19-22). She was defiled, destitute, discouraged, and desperate; but she came to Jesus and her need was met.

Her faith was almost superstitious, but the Lord honored it. She knew that He had healed others and she wanted Him to heal her. She could have used many excuses—the crowd was pressing around Him; nothing had worked for twelve years; it was not right to come to Jesus as a last resort; she was not an important person; He was on His way to heal Jairus' daughter—but she allowed nothing to stand in her way.

Jewish men wore tassels of blue twisted cords on the corners of their outer garments, as a reminder that they were to obey God's commandments (Num. 15:37-40; Deut. 22:12). The Pharisees went to extremes in obeying this rule to impress people with their sanctity (Matt. 23:5). Why the woman chose to touch this part of His garment, we do not know, but Jesus knew somebody with faith had touched Him and had been healed by His power. The healing was immediate and complete.

Why did the Lord ask her to give witness publicly? Was this not an embarrassment to her? Not in the least. To begin with, this public confession was for her sake. It was an opportunity for her to confess Christ and glorify God. Had she stolen away in the crowd, she would not have met Jesus personally or heard His words of assurance and comfort (v. 48).

But her confession was also an encouragement to Jairus, who would soon hear that his daughter had died. (Perhaps he wanted to blame the woman for the delay!) The woman's twelve years of trial were ended, and the same Christ who helped her would help Jairus. She was a testimony to the power of faith. True, she did not exercise "great faith," but Christ honored it and healed her body.

Finally, her witness was a rebuke to the multitude. You can be a part of the crowd and never get any blessing from being near Jesus! It is one thing to "press Him" and another thing to "touch Him" by faith. We may not have strong faith, but we do have a strong Saviour, and He responds even to a touch at the hem of His garment.

When the inventor of chloroform, Sir James Simpson, was dying, a friend said to him, "You will soon be resting on His bosom." Simpson humbly replied, "I don't know as I can do that, but I think I have hold of the hem of His garment."

Death (vv. 49-56). The ruler of a synagogue was the elder in charge of the public services and the care of the facilities. He saw to it that people were appointed to pray, read the Scriptures and give the sermon. He presided over the elders of the synagogue and was usually a man of reputation and wealth. It took a great deal of humility and courage for Jairus to approach Jesus and ask His help, for by this time the Jewish religious leaders were plotting to kill Him.

When Jairus left home, his daughter was so sick she was ready to die. By the time Jesus got away from the crowd to go with him, the girl had died. Jairus' friends thought that Jesus could help only living people, so they advised Jairus to drop the matter and come home. But Jesus encouraged the distraught father with a word of hope.

The scene at the home would have discouraged anybody! The professional mourners were already there, weeping and wailing; and a crowd of friends and neighbors had gathered. Jewish people in that day lost no time or energy in showing and sharing their grief. The body of the deceased would be buried that same day, after being washed and anointed.

Jesus took command of the situation and told the crowd to stop weeping because the girl was not dead but asleep. Of course she was dead, for her spirit had left her body (v. 55 with James 2:26); but to Jesus, death was only sleep. This image is often used in the New Testament to describe the death of believers (John 11:11-14; Acts 7:59-60; 1 Cor. 15:51; 1 Thes. 4:13-18). Sleep is a normal experience that we do not fear, and we should not fear death. It is the body that sleeps, not the spirit, for the spirit of the believer goes to be with Christ (Phil. 1:20-24; 2 Cor. 5:6-8). At the resurrection, the body will be "awakened" and glorified, and God's people will share the image of Christ (1 John 3:1-2).

The mourners laughed at Jesus because they knew the girl

was dead and that death was final. But they failed to realize that Jesus is "the resurrection and the life" (John 11:25-26). Had He not raised the widow's son from the dead? Did He not tell John the Baptist that the dead were being raised (7:22)? Apparently the mourners did not believe these reports and thought Jesus was a fool.

So He put them all out! This situation was much too tender and special for Him to allow dozens of unbelieving spectators to watch. He took the parents and three of His disciples, Peter, James, and John; and together they entered the room where the little girl lay dead.

He took her by the hand and spoke in Aramaic, "Talitha cumi! Little girl, arise!" (Peter would one day say "Tabitha cumi!"—Acts 9:40.) This was not a magic formula but a word of command from the Lord of life and death (Rev. 1:17-18). Her spirit returned to her body and she arose and began to walk around the room! Jesus told them to give her something to eat, for it is likely that during her illness she had eaten little or nothing. Jesus also instructed them not to spread the news, but still the word got around (Matt. 9:26).

Resurrection is a picture of the way Jesus Christ saves lost sinners and raises them from spiritual death (John 5:24; Eph. 2:1-10). The Gospels record three such resurrections, though Jesus probably performed more. In each instance, the person raised gave evidence of life. The widow's son began to speak (7:15), Jairus' daughter walked and ate food, and Lazarus was loosed from the graveclothes (John 11:44). When a lost sinner is raised from the dead, you can tell it by his speech, his walk, his appetite, and his "change of clothes" (Col. 3:1ff). You cannot hide life!

Peter, James, and John accompanied Jesus on three special occasions; and this was the first. The second was on the Mount of Transfiguration (9:28ff), and the third was in the Garden of Gethsemane (Mark 14:33ff). Campbell Morgan has pointed out that each of these events has something to do with death and that the three disciples learned from these experiences some valuable lessons about Jesus and death.

In the home of Jairus, they learned that Jesus is victorious over death. On the Mount of Transfiguration, they discovered that He would be glorified in His death; and in the Garden, they saw that He was surrendered to death. James was the first of the Twelve to die (Acts 12:1-2), John the last to die, and Peter's death was predicted by Jesus (John 21:18-19; 2 Peter 1:13-21). All three men needed these lessons, and we need them today.

8

A Many-Sided Ministry

Luke 9

It was an exasperating evening. I was studying and writing, and the phone was ringing every half-hour. Had the calls been from friends, I would have enjoyed taking a break and chatting, but they came from people wanting to sell me everything from dance tickets to investments. By the time I got to bed that night, I had just about decided to get an unlisted number and start protecting my privacy.

At 11 o'clock, a man phoned who was contemplating committing suicide; and with the Lord's help, I was able to encourage him to get a new grip on life. When I hung up, I gave thanks that I did not have an unlisted number. As I lay down to go back to sleep, I thought of the Lord Jesus and the kind of schedule He must have had. He was available to all kinds of people at all times, and He did not turn anyone away. He probably would not have had an unlisted number.

In this chapter, Dr. Luke described the busy life of the compassionate Son of Man as He performed four ministries.

1. Sending (9:1-11)

The commission (vv. 1-6). The Twelve had been ordained

some months before (6:13-16) and had been traveling with Jesus as His helpers. Now He was going to send them out in pairs (Mark 6:7) to have their own ministry and to put into practice what they had learned. This was their "solo flight."

But before He sent them out, He gave them the equipment needed to get the job done, as well as the instructions to follow. The parallel passage in Matthew 10 reveals that the Twelve were sent only to the people of Israel (vv. 5-6). Luke does not mention this since he wrote primarily for the Gentiles and emphasized the worldwide outreach of the Gospel.

Power is the ability to accomplish a task, and *authority* is the right to do it, and Jesus gave both to His apostles. They were able to cast out demons and heal the sick, but the most important ministry He gave them was that of preaching the Gospel. The word *preach* in verse 6 describes a herald proclaiming a message from the king, and in verse 6 it means "to preach the Good News." They were heralds of the Good News!

The apostles' ability to heal was a special gift that authenticated their ministry (see Rom. 15:18-19; 2 Cor. 12:12; Heb. 2:1-4). Miracles were one evidence that the Lord had sent them and was working through them (Mark 16:20). Today we test a person's ministry by the truth of the Word of God (1 John 2:18-29; 4:1-6). Miracles alone are not proof that a person is truly sent of God, for Satan can enable his false ministers to do amazing things (Matt. 24:24; 2 Cor. 11:13-15; 2 Thes. 2:9-10).

Jesus told the apostles what to take on their journey, with an emphasis on urgency and simplicity. They were not to take a "begging bag" along but were to trust God to open up homes for their hospitality. Matthew 10:11-15 tells how they were to select these homes. If they were refused, they should shake off the dust from their feet, a familiar act performed by orthodox Jews whenever they left Gentile territory (see Acts 13:51 and Luke 10:10-11).

The confusion (vv. 7-9). When the disciples left, Jesus also departed and ministered for a time in Galilee (Matt. 11:1); and together they attracted a great deal of attention. In fact, their work was even discussed in the highest levels of government! Herod Antipas (3:1) was a son of Herod the Great and the man who had John the Baptist killed (3:19-20; Matt. 14:1-12).

Who was this miracle worker? John the Baptist had done no miracles (John 10:41), but that might change if he were raised from the dead. The Jews expected Elijah to come, so perhaps the prophecy was being fulfilled (see Mal. 4:5; Luke 1:17; Matt. 11:10-14; 17:11-13). Herod's conscience was no doubt convicting him, and he was wondering if perhaps God had sent John back to judge him.

Herod kept trying to see Jesus; but Jesus, unlike some modern "religious celebrities," did not make it a point to go out of His way to mingle with the high and mighty. Jesus called the evil king a "fox" and was not intimidated by his threats (13:31-32). When Herod and Jesus did finally meet, the king hoped to see a miracle, but the Son of God did nothing and said nothing to him. Evil King Herod had silenced God's voice to him (23:6-12).

The conclusion (vv. 10-11). The apostles returned and gave a glowing report of their ministry, and Jesus suggested that they all take some time off for rest (Mark 6:30-32). As the popular speaker Vance Havner used to say, "If we don't come apart and rest, we'll just come apart." Their mission of preaching and healing had been demanding and they all needed time alone for physical and spiritual renewal. This is a good example for busy (and sometimes overworked) Christian workers to imitate.

Attracted by the signs Jesus was doing, the crowds would not leave Him alone, but followed Him from the cities. When Jesus and the Twelve landed, the crowd was already there to meet them, and Jesus had compassion on them and ministered to them (Matt. 14:13-14). The Son of Man could not even take a day off!

2. Feeding (9:12-17)

Our Lord was not the kind of person who could teach the Word and then say to hungry people, "Depart in peace, be ye warm and filled" (James 2:16). The disciples were only too eager to see the crowd leave (18:15, and see Matt. 15:23). They had not yet caught the compassion of Christ and the burden He had for the multitudes, but one day they would.

When you combine all four accounts of this miracle, you find that Jesus first asked Philip where they could buy enough bread to feed such a great crowd. (There could well have been 10,000 people there.) He was only testing Philip, "for He Himself knew what He was intending to do" (John 6:6, NASB). In the crisis hours of life, when your resources are low and your responsibilities are great, it is good to remember that God already has the problem solved.

Jesus started with what they had, a few loaves and fishes that were generously donated by a lad found by Andrew (John 6:8-9). Did Andrew know the boy? Or did the boy offer his little lunch without being asked? Before we ask God to do the impossible, let's start with the possible and give Him what we have. And while we are at it, let's give thanks for mothers who give their sons something to give to Jesus.

The Lord looked up to heaven, the source of our daily bread (Matt. 6:11), gave thanks, and blessed the food; and then He multiplied the few loaves and fishes. Jesus was the "producer" and His disciples were the "distributors." The amazing thing is that *everybody* was served and satisfied, and there were twelve baskets of leftovers, one for each of the disciples. Jesus takes good care of His servants.

This miracle was more than an act of mercy for hungry people, although that was important. It was also a sign of our Lord's Messiahship and an illustration of God's gracious provision for man's salvation. The next day, Jesus preached a sermon on "the bread of life" and urged the people to receive Him just as they had received the bread (John 6:22-59). But the people were more interested in their stomachs than their souls, and completely missed the spiritual impact of the miracle. Their desire was to make Jesus king so He could give them bread for the rest of their lives! (John 6:14-15)

After Jesus returned to heaven, the disciples must often have been encouraged by remembering this miracle. It teaches us to have compassion, to look upon problems as opportunities for God to work, and to give Him all that we have and trust Him to meet the needs. If we do all we can, He will step in and do the rest. "Let God's promises shine on your problems," said Corrie Ten Boom, and that is good counsel for us.

3. Teaching (9:18-36)

In Luke's Gospel, the feeding of the 5,000 marks the end of what is called "The Great Galilean Ministry" (4:14–9:17). Jesus now begins His journey to Jerusalem (see v. 51; and 13:22; 17:11; 18:31; and 19:11, 28). This would be a time of relative retirement with His disciples as He prepared them for what lay ahead. There is a parallel between this account and the account in Acts of Paul's last journey to Jerusalem. In both books we have "a tale of two cities": in Luke, from Nazareth to Jerusalem; and in Acts, from Jerusalem to Rome.

In this section, you see Jesus teaching them three basic lessons about His person, His sacrifice, and His kingdom.

His person (vv. 18-21). If any of us asked our friends what people were saying about us, it would be an evidence of pride, but not so with Jesus Christ. People had better know who He is, because what we think about Jesus determines our eternal destiny (John 8:24; 1 John 4:1-3). It is impossible to be wrong about Jesus and right with God.

Jesus had prayed all night before choosing His disciples (6:12-13), and now He prayed before asking for their personal confession of faith. The crowd would have its opinions (see vv. 7-8), but His disciples must have convictions. Peter was the spokesman for the group and gave a clear witness to the deity of Jesus Christ. This was the second time that he confessed Christ publicly (John 6:68-69). Except for Judas (John 6:70-71), all of the Twelve had faith in Jesus Christ.

Jesus commanded them (the word means "an order from a military officer") not to spread this truth openly. To begin with, the message of His Messiahship could not be divorced from the fact of His death and resurrection, and He was now going to teach this to the Twelve. They had a difficult time grasping this new lesson and did not really understand it until after He was raised from the dead (24:44-48). The Jewish people saw Jesus primarily as a healer and a potential deliverer. If the apostles began preaching that He was indeed the Messiah, it might cause a popular uprising against Rome.

His sacrifice (vv. 22-26). Jesus had already given a number of "hints" about His sacrificial death, but now He began to teach this truth clearly to His disciples. John the Baptist had presented Him as the "Lamb of God" (John 1:29), and Jesus had predicted the "destruction" of the temple of His body (John 2:19). When He compared Himself to the serpent in the wilderness (John 3:14) and to Jonah (Matt. 12:38-40), Jesus was making statements about His suffering and death.

This is the first of three statements in Luke about His coming passion in Jerusalem (9:43-45; 18:31-34). It is clear that the Twelve did not understand, partly because of their unbelief and immaturity, and partly because it was "hidden" from them by God. Jesus taught them as they were able to receive the truth (John 16:12). It must have shocked the men to hear that their own religious leaders would kill their Master.

But Jesus did not stop with a private announcement of His own death. He also made a public declaration about a cross for *every* disciple. In his Gospel, Matthew tells us that this was necessary because of Peter's desire to protect Jesus from suffering (16:22ff). Keep in mind that Jesus is talking about *discipleship* and not *sonship*. We are not saved from our sins because we take up a cross and follow Jesus, but because we trust the Saviour who died on the cross for our sins. After we become children of God, then we can become disciples.

The closest contemporary word to "disciple" is probably "apprentice." A disciple is more than a student who learns lessons by means of lectures and books. He is one who learns by living and working with his teacher in a daily "hands on" experience. Too many Christians are content to be listeners who gain a lot of knowledge but who have never put that knowledge into practice.

In the Roman world, the cross was a symbol of shame, guilt, suffering, and rejection. There could be no more despicable way to die. Crucifixion was not mentioned in polite conversation, and the people would no more think of wearing crosses on their person than we would think of wearing gold or silver electric chairs. Jesus laid down the stern requirements for discipleship. We must first "say no" to ourselves—not simply to pleasures or possessions, but to *self*—and then take up *our* cross and follow Christ daily. This means to be identified with Him in surrender, suffering, and sacrifice. You cannot crucify yourself; you can only yield your body (Rom. 12:1-2) and let God do the rest.

Of course, this kind of life seems foolish to the world; but to the Christian, it is wisdom. To save your life is to lose it, and how can you ever get it back again? But to give your life to Christ is to save it and to live it in fullness. If a person owned the whole world, he would still be too poor to buy back a lost life.

Discipleship is a daily discipline: we follow Jesus a step at a time, a day at a time. A weary cleaning woman said to a friend of mine, "The trouble with life is that it's so daily!" But she was wrong. One of the *best* things about life is that we can take it a day at a time (Deut. 33:25).

Our motive should be to glorify Christ. Anyone who is ashamed of Christ will never take up a cross and follow Him. But if we are ashamed of Him now, He will be ashamed of us when He comes again (Mark 8:38; 2 Tim. 2:11-13) and we will be ashamed before Him (1 John 2:28).

His kingdom (vv. 27-36). As far as the Gospel record is concerned, the Transfiguration was the only occasion during Christ's earthly ministry when He revealed the glory of His person. Luke did not use the word *transfigure* but he described the same scene (Matt. 17:2; Mark 9:2). The word means "a change in appearance that comes from within," and it gives us the English word *metamorphosis.*

What were the reasons behind this event? For one thing, it was God's seal of approval to Peter's confession of faith that Jesus is the Son of God (John 1:14). It was also the Father's way of encouraging the Son as He began to make His way to Jerusalem. The Father had spoken at the baptism (3:22) and would speak again during that final week of the Son's earthly ministry (John 12:23-28). Beyond the suffering of the cross would be the glory of the throne, a lesson that Peter emphasized in his First Epistle (4:12–5:4).

Our Lord's own words in 9:27 indicate that the event was a demonstration (or illustration) of the promised kingdom of God. This seems logical, for the disciples were confused about the kingdom because of Jesus' words about the cross. (We must not be too hard on them because the prophets were also confused—1 Peter 1:10-12.) Jesus was reassuring them that the Old Testament prophecies would be fulfilled, but first He had to suffer before He could enter into His glory (note especially 2 Peter 1:12-21).

But there is also a practical lesson here, for we can have a spiritual "transfiguration" experience each day as we walk with the Lord. Romans 12:1-2 and 2 Corinthians 3:18 tell us how. As we surrender body, mind, and will, the Lord transforms us from within so that we are not conformed to the world. As we behold Him in the Word (the mirror), we are "transfigured" by the Spirit "from glory to glory." The theological name for this experience is *sanctification,* the process by which we become more like the Lord Jesus Christ, which is the Father's goal for each of His children (Rom. 8:19; 1 John 3:2). Note that our Lord was once again praying, which suggests that prayer is one of the keys to a transformed life.

Peter, James, and John had accompanied Jesus when He raised Jairus' daughter from the dead (8:51ff), and they would accompany Him when He prayed in the Garden (Matt. 26:36-46). These three occasions remind me of Philippians 3:10, "That I may know Him [the Transfiguration], and the power of His resurrection [raising the girl], and the fellowship of His sufferings [in the Garden]."

This may well have been the greatest "Bible conference" ever held on earth! Even apart from the great glory that was involved, here you certainly had the greatest speakers: Moses, the Law; Elijah, the prophets; and Jesus, who came to fulfill the Law and the prophets. You had the greatest topic: Jesus' "decease" (the Greek is *exodus*) that He would accomplish at Jerusalem. Moses had led Israel out of bondage to Egypt, and Elijah had delivered them from bondage to false gods; but Jesus would die to set *a sinful world* free from bondage to sin and death (Gal. 1:4; Col. 1:13; Heb. 2:14-15).

And while all of this was going on, the three privileged disciples were sleeping! (They would repeat this failure in the Garden.) Peter's suggestion reminds us of the Jewish "Feast of Booths" that in the Bible is related to the future kingdom (Lev. 23:33-44; Zech. 14:16-21). Peter wanted Jesus to hold on to the glory *apart from the suffering,* but this is not God's plan.

The Father interrupted Peter by bathing the scene in a cloud of glory (Ex. 13:21-22; 40:35, 38) and speaking out of the cloud. (Peter would one day be interrupted by the Son [Matt. 17:24-27] and by the Spirit [Acts 10:44].) These arresting words from heaven remind us of Deuteronomy 18:15;

Psalm 2:7; and Isaiah 42:1. When the cloud was gone, Elijah and Moses were also gone.

As wonderful as these experiences are, they are not the basis for a consistent Christian life. That can come only through the Word of God. Experiences come and go, but the Word remains. Our recollection of past experiences will fade, but God's Word never changes. The farther we get from these events, the less impact they make on our lives. That was why the Father said "Hear Him!" and why Peter made this same emphasis on the Word in his report (2 Peter 1:12-21). Our own personal "transfiguration" comes from inner renewal (Rom. 12:1-2), and that comes from the Word (2 Cor. 3:18).

4. Enduring (9:37-62)

"How long shall I stay with you and put up with you?" (v. 41, NIV) You might expect that lament to come from an over-worked kindergarten teacher, or an impatient army drill instructor, but it was made by the sinless Son of God! We are prone to forget how long-suffering our Lord had to be while He was ministering on earth, especially with His own disciples.

When you analyze this section of Luke's Gospel, you can better understand why Jesus spoke those words: *He was grieved over the failures of His followers.* He had given His apostles authority over Satan, yet they were too weak to cast out a demon (vv. 37-45). In feeding the 5,000, Jesus gave them an example of compassion, yet they persisted in manifesting selfishness and lack of love (vv. 46-56). He taught clearly what it meant to follow Him, yet the volunteers turned out to be "me first" disciples (vv. 57-62). No wonder He was grieved!

Lack of power (vv. 37-45). We dare not stay on the glorious mountaintop when there are battles to fight in the valley below. Here was another "only child" needing the help of the Lord (7:12; 8:42), and even more so because His own disciples had failed. They had the power and the authority (v. 1) but they did not have the success. Why?

When you study all three reports (Matt. 17; Mark 9), you discover what was lacking in their lives. First on the list was *faith* (Matt. 17:19-20); they were part of an unbelieving generation and had lost the confidence that they needed in order to use their power. But *prayer* and *fasting* were also lacking (Mark 9:29), which indicates that the nine men had allowed their devotional disciplines to erode during their Lord's brief absence. No matter what spiritual gifts we may have, their exercise is never automatic.

The devil tried one last throw (a wrestling term in the Greek), but Jesus rebuked the demon and cast him out. The Lord lovingly gave the boy back to his father (see 7:15) and then took the Twelve aside for another lesson about the Cross. After all, it was at the cross that Jesus would give Satan that final blow of defeat (John 12:31-32; Col. 2:15).

Lack of love (vv. 46-56). The disciples did not have much love for each other, or they would not have argued over who was the greatest (vv. 46-48). Perhaps this debate started because of envy (three of the disciples had been with Jesus on the mount), or because of pride (the other nine had failed to cast out the demon). Also, just before this, Jesus had paid Peter's temple tax for him (Matt. 17:24-27); and this may have aroused some envy.

In His kingdom, the example of greatness is a little child—helpless, dependent, without status, living by faith. The only thing worse than a child trying to act like an adult is an adult acting like a child! There is a great difference between being childlike and childish! (See 1 Cor. 13:4-5 and 14:20.)

They also showed a lack of love for believers outside their own group (vv. 49-50). This is what we would expect from a "son of thunder" (Mark 3:17)! Perhaps John was trying to impress Jesus with his zeal for protecting His name, but the Lord was not impressed. Believers who think that their group is the only group God recognizes and blesses are in for a shock when they get to heaven.

Nor did the apostles love their enemies (vv. 51-56). James and John had seen the Prophet Elijah on the mount, so they thought they might imitate him and call down fire from heaven (2 Kings 1)! The Samaritans and Jews had been enemies for centuries (2 Kings 17:24-41), so it was understandable that this village would reject Jesus as He traveled toward Jerusalem (John 4:9, 20). Jesus rebuked their vengeful spirit and simply went to another village (Matt. 5:37-48). Later, Samaria would be reached with the Gospel (Acts 8).

Lack of discipline (vv. 57-62). Three men could have become disciples, but they would not meet the conditions that Jesus laid down. The first man was a scribe (Matt. 8:19) who volunteered to go until he heard the cost: he had to deny himself. Apparently he was accustomed to a comfortable home.

The second man was called by Jesus (what an honor!), but he was rejected because he would not take up the cross and die to self. He was worried about somebody else's funeral when he should have been planning his own! Jesus is not suggesting here that we dishonor our parents, but only that we not permit our love for family to weaken our love for the Lord. We should love Christ so much that our love for family would look like hatred in comparison (14:26).

The third man also volunteered, but he could not follow Christ because he was looking back instead of ahead. There is nothing wrong with a loving farewell (1 Kings 19:19-21), but if it gets in the way of obedience, it becomes sin. Jesus saw that this man's heart was not wholly with Him, but that he would be plowing and looking back (see Gen. 19:17, 26; Phil. 3:13-14).

No wonder the laborers are few! (Luke 10:2)

It would appear that what Jesus taught His disciples and the multitudes had done them little good. They lacked power, love, and discipline, and they grieved His heart. If we today lack these spiritual essentials, we can never truly be His disciples, but they are available to us from the Lord. "For God did not give us a spirit of timidity, but of power, of love and of self-discipline" (2 Tim. 1:7, NIV).

Are we a joy to Jesus Christ, or are we breaking His heart?

9

What in the World Does a Christian Do?

Luke 10

The three scenes in chapter 10 illustrate the threefold ministry of every Christian believer, and they answer the question, "What in the world does a Christian do?"

To begin with, we are the Lord's *ambassadors,* sent to represent Him in this world (vv. 1-24). We are also *neighbors,* looking for opportunities to show mercy in the name of Christ (vv. 25-37). But at the heart of all our ministry is devotion to Christ, so we must be *worshipers* who take time to listen to His Word and commune with Him (vv. 38-42).

Whether we are in the harvest field, on the highway, or in the home, our highest privilege and our greatest joy is to do the will of God.

1. Ambassadors: Representing the Lord (10:1-24)

This event should not be confused with the sending out of the Twelve (9:1-11; Matt. 10). There are similarities in the charges given, but this is to be expected since both groups were sent by the same Master to do the same basic job. The twelve apostles ministered throughout Galilee, but these men were sent into Judea, and the men in this chapter are not called apostles. They were anonymous disciples.

Why is this event recorded only by Luke, and why did Jesus select seventy men instead of some other number? (Some texts say seventy-two, and the textual evidence is about even.) Just as the Twelve were associated in number with the twelve sons of Jacob and the twelve tribes of Israel, so the Seventy may be associated with the seventy nations listed in Genesis 10. Luke's emphasis is on the universality of the Gospel message, so it seems reasonable that he would be led by the Holy Spirit to include this event. It was a symbolic way of saying, "Jesus wants the message spread to all nations."

The explanation (vv. 1-12). These men were not called "apostles," but they were still "sent *[apostello]* with a commission" to represent the Lord. They were therefore truly ambassadors of the King. Not only were they sent *by* Him, but they were also sent *before* Him to prepare the way for His coming. Their calling was certainly a dignified one.

It was also a difficult calling (v. 2). Harvesting is hard work, even when there are many people helping you, but these men were sent into a vast field with very few workers to help them reap a great harvest. Instead of praying for an easier job, they were to pray for more laborers to join them, and we today need to pray that same prayer. (Please note that it is *laborers*, not spectators, who pray for more laborers! Too many Christians are praying for somebody else to do a job they are unwilling to do themselves.)

Their calling was a dangerous one. As they invaded enemy territory (v. 17), they would be like "lambs among wolves" (v. 3). But as long as they relied on the Lord, they would win the battle. "Any man who takes Jesus Christ seriously becomes the target of the devil," Vance Havner often told audiences. "Most church members do not give Satan enough trouble to arouse his opposition."

It would require discipline and faith for them to do the job (vv. 4-8). There was an urgency about the work, and the Lord did not want them to be overburdened with extra supplies or be delayed on the road by elaborate Eastern greetings. They had to trust God to provide homes and food for them, and they were not to be embarrassed to accept hospitality. After all, they were laboring for the Lord and bringing blessing into the home, and "the laborer is worthy of his hire" (v. 7; see also 1 Cor. 9:14 and 1 Tim. 5:18).

They were ambassadors of peace, bringing healing to the sick, deliverance to the possessed, and the Good News of salvation to lost sinners. Like Joshua's army of old, they first proclaimed peace to the cities. If a city rejected the offer of peace, then it chose judgment (Deut. 20:10-18). It is a serious thing to reject the ambassadors God sends.

It is important to note that the special power that Jesus gave to His apostles (9:1) and to the Seventy is not ours to claim today. These two preaching missions were very special ministries, and God did not promise to duplicate them in our age. Our Lord's commission to us emphasizes the proclamation of the message, not the performing of miracles (Matt. 28:19-20; Luke 24:46-49).

Denunciation (vv. 13-16). This seems like harsh language from the lips of the Son of God, but we dare not ignore it or try to explain it away. He named three ancient cities that had been judged by God—Sodom (Gen. 19), and Tyre and Sidon (Ezek. 26–28; Isa. 23)—and used them to warn three cities of His day: Chorazin, Bethsaida, and Capernaum. These three cities had been given more privileges than the three ancient cities, and therefore they had more responsibility. If Sodom, Tyre, and Sidon were destroyed, how could Chorazin, Bethsaida, and Capernaum escape?

To hear Christ's ambassadors means to hear Him, and to despise His representatives means to despise Him. "As My Father hath sent Me, even so send I you" (John 20:21; see also 2 Cor. 5:18-21). The way a nation treats an ambassador is the way it treats the government the ambassador represents. For an interesting illustration of this truth, read 2 Samuel 10.

Jubilation (vv. 17-24). There is a threefold joy here: the joy of service (vv. 17-19), the joy of salvation (v. 20), and the joy of sovereignty (vv. 21-24).

We can well understand the joy of the Seventy as they returned to report their victories to Jesus. He had given them power and authority to heal, to cast out demons and to preach the Word, and they were successful! In the midst of their great joy, they were careful to give God the glory ("in Thy name").

They had seen individual victories from city to city, but Jesus saw these victories as part of a war that dethroned and defeated Satan (note Isa. 14:4-23; John 12:31-32; and Rev. 12:8-9). As believers, we are weak in ourselves, but we can be "strong in the Lord, and in the power of His might" (Eph. 6:10ff). Each victory is important to the Lord, no matter how insignificant it may seem in our eyes. Satan will not finally be judged until Jesus casts him into the lake of fire (Rev. 20:10), but God's people can today claim Christ's Calvary victory by faith (Col. 2:15).

But the enemy will not give up! Satan would certainly attack Christ's servants and seek to destroy them. That is why our Lord added the words of encouragement in v. 19. He assured them that their authority was not gone now that the preaching mission had ended, and that they could safely tread on the "old serpent" without fear (Rev. 12:9; Gen. 3:15).

The Lord cautioned them not to "go on rejoicing" over their victories but to rejoice because their names had been written in heaven. (The verb means "they have been written and they stand written." It is a statement of assurance. See Revelation 20:12-15; Philippians 4:3.) As wonderful as their miracles were, the greatest miracle of all is still the salvation of a lost soul. The Greek word translated "written" means "to inscribe formally and solemnly." It was used for the signing of a will, a marriage document, or a peace treaty, and also for the enrolling of a citizen. The perfect tense in the Greek means "it stands written."

But our highest joy is not found in service or even in our salvation, but in being submitted to the sovereign will of the Heavenly Father, for this is the foundation for both service and salvation. Here we see God the Son rejoicing through God the Holy Spirit because of the will of God the Father! "I delight to do Thy will, O my God" (Ps. 40:8).

Jesus was not rejoicing because sinners were blind to God's truth, for God is "not willing that any should perish" (2 Peter 3:9). He rejoiced because *the understanding of that truth* did not depend on natural abilities or education. If that were the case, most of the people in the world would be shut out of the kingdom. When the Twelve and the Seventy were preaching, they did not see the "wise and learned" humbling themselves to receive God's truth and grace, but they saw the "common people" trusting the Word (7:29-30; 1 Cor. 1:26-29). In His sovereign will, God has ordained that sinners must humble themselves before they can be lifted up (1 Peter 5:6; James 4:6).

Christ's ambassadors were indeed privileged people. They were able to see and hear things that the greatest saints in the Old Testament ages yearned to see and hear but could not. The Messiah was at work, and they were a part of His work!

2. Neighbors: Imitating the Lord (10:25-37)

It was expected that rabbis would discuss theological matters in public, and the question this scribe (lawyer) asked was one that was often debated by the Jews. It was a good question asked with a bad motive, because the lawyer hoped to trap our Lord. However, Jesus trapped the lawyer!

Our Lord sent the man back to the Law, not because the Law saves us (Gal. 2:16, 21; 3:21), but because the Law shows us that we need to be saved. There can be no real conversion without conviction, and the Law is what God uses to convict sinners (Rom. 3:20).

The scribe gave the right answer, but he would not apply it personally to himself and admit his own lack of love for both God and his neighbor. So, instead of *being justified* by throwing himself on the mercy of God (18:9-14), he tried to *justify himself* and wriggle out of his predicament. He used the old debating tactic, "Define your terms! What do you mean by 'neighbor'? Who is my neighbor?"

Jesus did not say that this story was a parable, so it could well be the report of an actual occurrence. For Jesus to tell a story that made the Jews look bad and the Samaritans look good would either be dangerous or self-defeating. "You just made that up!" they could say. "We all know that nothing like that would ever happen!" So it is possible that some of His listeners, including the lawyer, knew that such a thing had really happened. Either way, the account is realistic.

The worst thing we can do with any parable, especially this one, is turn it into an allegory and make everything stand for something. The victim becomes the lost sinner who is half dead (alive physically, dead spiritually), helplessly left on the road of life. The priest and Levite represent the law and the sacrifices, neither of which can save the sinner.

The Samaritan is Jesus Christ who saves the man, pays the bill, and promises to come again. The inn stands for the local church where believers are cared for, and the "two pence" are the two ordinances, baptism and communion. If you take this approach to Scripture, you can make the Bible say almost anything you please, and you are sure to miss the messages God wants you to get.

The road from Jerusalem down to Jericho was indeed a dangerous one. Since the temple workers used it so much, you would have thought the Jews or Romans would have taken steps to make it safe. It is much easier to maintain a religious system than it is to improve the neighborhood.

Most of us can think up excuses for the priest and Levite as they ignored the victim. (Maybe we have used them ourselves!) The priest had been serving God at the temple all week and was anxious to get home. Perhaps the bandits were still lurking in the vicinity and using the victim as "bait." Why take a chance? Anyway, it was not his fault that the man was attacked. The road was busy, so somebody else was bound to come along and help the man. The priest left it to the Levite, and then the Levite did what the priest did—nothing! Such is the power of the bad example of a religious man.

By using a Samaritan as the hero, Jesus disarmed the Jews, for the Jews and Samaritans were enemies (John 4:9 and 8:48). It was not a Jew helping a Samaritan but a Samaritan helping a Jew *who had been ignored by his fellow Jews!* The Samaritan loved those who hated him, risked his own life, spent his own money (two days' wages for a laborer), and was never publicly rewarded or honored as far as we know.

What the Samaritan did helps us better understand what it means to "show mercy" (v. 37), and it also illustrates the ministry of Jesus Christ. The Samaritan identified with the needs of the stranger and had compassion on him. There was no logical reason why he should rearrange his plans and spend his money just to help an "enemy" in need, but mercy does not need reasons. Being an expert in the law, the scribe certainly knew that God required His people to show mercy, even to strangers and enemies (Lev. 19:33-34; Ex. 23:4-5; Micah 6:8).

See how wisely Jesus "turned the tables" on the lawyer. Trying to evade responsibility, the man asked, "Who is my neighbor?" But Jesus asked, "Which of these three men was neighbor to the victim?" The big question is, "To whom can I be a neighbor?" and this has nothing to do with geography, citizenship, or race. Wherever people need us, there we can be neighbors and, like Jesus Christ, show mercy.

The lawyer wanted to discuss "neighbor" in a general way, but Jesus forced him to consider a specific man in need. How easy it is for us to talk about abstract ideals and fail to help solve concrete problems. We can discuss things like "poverty" and "job opportunities" and yet never personally help feed a hungry family or help somebody find a job.

Of course, the lawyer wanted to make the issue somewhat complex and philosophical, but Jesus made it simple and practical. He moved it from *duty* to *love*, from *debating* to *doing*. To be sure, our Lord was not condemning discussions or debates; He was only warning us not to use these things as excuses for doing nothing. Committees are not always committed!

One of my favorite D.L. Moody stories illustrates this point. Attending a convention in Indianapolis, Mr. Moody asked singer Ira Sankey to meet him at 6 o'clock one evening at a certain street corner. When Sankey arrived, Mr. Moody put him on a box and asked him to sing, and it was not long before a crowd gathered. Moody spoke briefly, inviting the crowd to follow him to the nearby opera house. Before long, the auditorium was filled, and the evangelist preached the Gospel to the spiritually hungry people.

When the delegates to the convention started to arrive, Moody stopped preaching and said, "Now we must close as the brethren of the convention wish to come and to discuss the question, 'How to Reach the Masses.' " *Touché!*

We may read this passage and think only of "the high cost of caring," but it is far more costly *not* to care. The priest and the Levite lost far more by their neglect than the Samaritan did by his concern. They lost the opportunity to become better men and good stewards of what God had given them. They could have been a good influence in a bad world, but they chose to be a bad influence. *The Samaritan's one deed of mercy has inspired sacrificial ministry all over the world.* Never say that such ministry is wasted! God sees to it that no act of loving service in Christ's name is ever lost.

It all depends on your outlook. To the thieves, this traveling

Jew was a victim to exploit, so they attacked him. To the priest and Levite, he was a nuisance to avoid, so they ignored him. But to the Samaritan, he was a neighbor to love and help, so he took care of him. What Jesus said to the lawyer, He says to us: "Go and *keep on doing it* likewise" (literal translation).

3. Worshipers: Listening to the Lord (10:38-42)

Worship is at the heart of all that we are and all that we do in the Christian life. It is important that we be busy ambassadors, taking the message of the Gospel to lost souls. It is also essential to be merciful Samaritans, seeking to help exploited and hurting people who need God's mercy. But before we can represent Christ as we should, or imitate Him in our caring ministry, we must spend time with Him and learn from Him. We must "take time to be holy."

Mary of Bethany is seen three times in the Gospel record, and on each occasion, she is in the same place: at the feet of Jesus. She sat at His feet and listened to His Word (10:39), fell at His feet and shared her woe (John 11:32), and came to His feet and poured out her worship (John 12:3). It is interesting to note that in each of these instances, there is some kind of fragrance: in Luke 10, it is food; in John 11, it is death (v. 39); and in John 12, it is perfume.

Mary and Martha are often contrasted as though each believer must make a choice: be a *worker* like Martha or a *worshiper* like Mary. Certainly our personalities and gifts are different, but that does not mean that the Christian life is an either/or situation. Charles Welsey said it perfectly in one of his hymns:

> Faithful to my Lord's commands,
> I still would choose the better part;
> Serve with careful Martha's hands,
> And loving Mary's heart.

It seems evident that the Lord wants each of us to imitate Mary in our worship and Martha in our work. Blessed are the balanced!

Consider Martha's situation. She received Jesus into her home *and then neglected Him as she prepared an elaborate meal that He did not need!* Certainly a meal was in order, but what we do *with* Christ is far more important than what we do *for* Christ. Again, it is not an either/or situation; it is a matter of balance. Mary had done her share of the work in the kitchen and then had gone to "feed" on the Lord's teachings. Martha felt neglected after Mary left the kitchen, and she began to complain and to suggest that neither the Lord nor Mary really cared!

Few things are as damaging to the Christian life as trying to work for Christ without taking time to commune with Christ. "For without Me ye can do nothing" (John 15:5). Mary chose the better part, the part that could not be taken from her. She knew that she could not live "by bread alone" (Matt. 4:4).

Whenever we criticize others and pity ourselves because we feel overworked, we had better take time to examine our lives. Perhaps in all of our busyness, we have been ignoring the Lord. Martha's problem was not that she had too much work to do, but that she allowed her work to distract her and pull her apart. She was trying to serve two masters! If serving Christ makes us difficult to live with, then something is terribly wrong with our service!

The key is to have the right priorities: Jesus Christ must be first, then others, and then ourselves. It is vitally important that we spend time "at the feet of Jesus" every single day, letting Him share His Word with us. *The most important part of the Christian life is the part that only God sees.* Unless we meet Christ personally and privately each day, we will soon end up like Martha: busy but not blessed.

Often in my pastoral ministry, I have asked people with serious problems, "Tell me about your devotional life." The usual response has been an embarrassed look, a bowed head, and the quiet confession, "I stopped reading my Bible and praying a long time ago." And they wondered why they had problems!

According to John 12:1-2, Martha must have learned her lesson, for she prepared a feast for Jesus, the Twelve, and her brother and sister—that's fifteen people—*and did not utter one word of complaint!* She had God's peace in her heart because she had learned to sit at the feet of Jesus.

We are ambassadors, neighbors, and worshipers, these three; and the greatest of these is worshipers.

Blessed are the balanced.

10

Learning Life's Lessons

Luke 11

Our Lord's teaching in chapter 11 grew out of a prayer meeting, a miracle, and an invitation to dinner. Jesus used these occasions to give instructions about four important topics: prayer, Satan, spiritual opportunity, and hypocrisy. It is important that we today understand these topics and apply these truths to our own lives.

1. Prayer (11:1-13)

The priority of prayer (v. 1). We usually think of John the Baptist as a prophet and martyr, and yet our Lord's disciples remembered him as a man of prayer. John was a "miracle baby," filled with the Holy Spirit before he was born, and yet he had to pray. He was privileged to introduce the Messiah to Israel, and yet he had to pray. Jesus said that John was the greatest of the prophets (7:28), and yet John had to depend on prayer. If prayer was that vital to a man who had these many advantages, how much more important it ought to be to us who do not have these advantages!

John's disciples had to pray and Jesus' disciples wanted to learn better how to pray. They did not ask the Master to teach them how to preach or do great signs; they asked Him to teach them to pray. We today sometimes think that we would be better Christians if only we had been with Jesus when He was on earth, but this is not likely. The disciples were with Him and yet they failed many times! They could perform miracles, and yet they wanted to learn to pray.

But the greatest argument for the priority of prayer is the fact that our Lord was a Man of prayer. Thus far we have seen that He prayed at His baptism (3:21), before He chose the Twelve (6:12), when the crowds increased (5:16), before He asked the Twelve for their confession of faith (9:18), and at His Transfiguration (9:29). The disciples knew that He often prayed alone (Mark 1:35), and they wanted to learn from Him this secret of spiritual power and wisdom.

If Jesus Christ, the perfect Son of God, had to depend on prayer during "the days of His flesh" (Heb. 5:7), then how much more do you and I need to pray! Effective prayer is the provision for every need and the solution for every problem.

Pattern for prayer (vv. 2-4). We call this "The Lord's Prayer," not because Jesus prayed it (He never had to ask for forgiveness), but because Jesus taught it. There is nothing wrong with praying this prayer personally or as part of a congregation, so long as we do it from a believing heart that is sincere and submitted. How easy it is to "recite" these words and not really mean them, but that can happen even when we sing and preach! The fault lies with us, not with this prayer.

This is a "pattern prayer," given to guide us in our own praying (see Matt. 6:9-15 for the parallel). It teaches us that true prayer depends on a spiritual relationship with God that enables us to call Him "Father," and this can come only through faith in Jesus Christ (Rom. 8:14-17; Gal. 4:1-7).

Lyndon Johnson's press secretary, Bill Moyers, was saying grace at a staff lunch, and the President shouted, "Speak up, Bill! I can't hear a thing!" Moyers quietly replied, "I wasn't addressing you, Mr. President." It is good to remind ourselves that when we pray, we talk to God.

True prayer also involves *responsibilities:* honoring God's kingdom and doing God's will (v. 2). It has well been said that the purpose of prayer is not to get man's will done in heaven, but to get God's will done on earth. Prayer is not telling God what we want and then selfishly enjoying it. Prayer is asking God to use us to accomplish *what He wants* so that His name is glorified, His kingdom is extended and strengthened, and His will is done. I must test all of my personal requests by these overruling concerns if I expect God to hear and answer my prayers.

It is important for Christians to know the Word of God, for there we discover the will of God. We must never separate prayer and the Word (John 15:7). During my ministry, I have seen professed Christians disobey God and defend themselves by saying, "I prayed about it and God said it was all right!" This includes a girl who married an unsaved man (2 Cor. 6:14-18), a fellow living with a girl who was not his wife (1 Thes. 4:1-8), and a preacher who started his own church because all the other churches were wrong and only he had true "spiritual insight" (Phil. 2:1-16).

Once we are secure in our relationship with God and His will, then we can bring our *requests* to Him (vv. 3-4). We can ask Him to provide our needs (not our greeds!) for today, to forgive us for what we have done yesterday, and to lead us in the future. All of our needs may be included in these three requests: material and physical provision, moral and spiritual perfection, and divine protection and direction. If we pray this way, we can be sure of praying in God's will.

Persistence in prayer (vv. 5-8). In this parable, Jesus did not say that God is like this grouchy neighbor. In fact, He said just the opposite. If a tired and selfish neighbor finally meets the needs of a bothersome friend, how much more will a loving Heavenly Father meet the needs of His own dear children! He is arguing from the lesser to the greater.

We have already seen that prayer is based on *sonship* ("Our Father"), not on friendship; but Jesus used friendship to illustrate persistence in prayer. God the Father is not like this neighbor, for He never sleeps, never gets impatient or irritable, is always generous, and delights in meeting the needs of His children. The friend at the door had to keep on knocking in order to get what he needed, but God is quick to respond to His children's cries (18:1-8).

The argument is clear: if persistence finally paid off as a man beat on the door of a reluctant friend, how much more would persistence bring blessing as we pray to a loving Heavenly Father! After all, we are the children *in the house with Him!*

The word translated "importunity" means "shamelessness" or "avoidance of shame." It can refer to the man at the door who was not ashamed to wake up his friend, but it can also refer to the friend in the house. Hospitality to strangers is a basic law in the East (Gen. 18:1ff). If a person refused to entertain a guest, he brought disgrace on the whole village and the neighbors would have nothing to do with him. The man in the house knew this and did not want to embarrass himself, his family, or his village; so he got up and met the need.

Why does our Father in heaven answer prayer? Not just to meet the needs of His children, but to meet them in such a way that it brings glory to His name. "Hallowed be Thy name." *When God's people pray, God's reputation is at stake.* The way He takes care of His children is a witness to the world that He can be trusted. Phillips Brooks said that prayer is not overcoming God's reluctance; it is laying hold of His highest willingness. Persistence in prayer is not an attempt to change God's mind ("Thy will be done") but to get ourselves to the place where He can trust us with the answer.

Promises for prayer (vv. 9-13). The tenses of the verbs

are important here: "Keep on asking . . . keep on seeking . . . keep on knocking." In other words, *don't come to God only in the midnight emergencies, but keep in constant communion with your Father.* Jesus called this "abiding" (John 15:1ff), and Paul exhorted, "Pray without ceasing" (1 Thes. 5:17). As we pray, God will either answer or show us why He cannot answer. Then it is up to us to do whatever is necessary in our lives so that the Father can trust us with the answer.

Note that the lesson closes with an emphasis on God as Father (vv. 11-13). Because He knows us and loves us, *we never need to be afraid of the answers that He gives.* Again, Jesus argued from the lesser to the greater: if an earthly father gives what is best to his children, surely the Father in heaven will do even more. This even includes "the good things of the Holy Spirit" (v. 13 with Matt. 7:11), blessings that in the Old Testament were reserved only for a special few.

2. Satan (11:14-28)

Accusation (vv. 14-16). This is the third miracle of deliverance our Lord performed that elicited from His enemies the accusation that He was in league with Satan (see Matt. 9:32-34 and 12:22-37). Instead of rejoicing that God had sent a Redeemer, the religious leaders were rebelling against the truth of God's Word and seeking to discredit Christ's work and character. Imagine people being so blind that they could not distinguish a work of God from a work of Satan!

"Beelzebub" was one of the names of the Philistine god Baal (2 Kings 1:1-3); it means "lord of flies." A variant is "Beelzebul" which means "lord of the dwelling" and ties in with Christ's illustrations in verses 18-26. The Jews often used this name when referring to Satan.

The request in verse 16 was a part of the accusation. "If you are really working for God," they were saying in effect, "prove it by giving us a sign from heaven, not just a miracle on earth." They were tempting God, which is a dangerous thing to do.

Refutation (vv. 17-22). Jesus answered their charges with three arguments. First, their accusation was illogical. Why would Satan fight against himself and divide his own kingdom? (Note that Jesus believed in a real devil who has a kingdom that is strong and united. See Ephesians 2:1-3; 6:10ff.) Second, their charges were self-incriminating: by what power were the Jews casting out demons? How do their works differ from Christ's works? On the contrary, Christ's miracles show that the kingdom of *God* is present, not the kingdom of *Satan!*

Finally, their accusation was really an admission of His power, for He could not defeat Satan unless He were stronger than Satan. Jesus pictured Satan as a strong man in armor, guarding his palace and his goods. But Jesus invaded Satan's territory, destroyed his armor and weapons, and claimed his spoils! (See Col. 2:15; John 12:31-33; 1 John 3:8.) Our Lord has "led captivity captive" (Eph. 4:8) and set the prisoners free (Luke 4:18). Though he is permitted limited authority, Satan is a defeated enemy.

Application (vv. 23-28). It is impossible to be neutral in this spiritual war (v. 23; also see 9:50), for neutrality means standing against Him. There are two spiritual forces at work in the world, and we must choose between them. Satan is scattering and destroying, but Jesus Christ is gathering and building. We must make a choice, and if we choose to make *no* choice, we are really choosing against Him.

Jesus illustrated the danger of neutrality by telling the story of the man and the demon. The man's body was the demon's "house" (v. 24, and note vv. 17 and 21). For some unknown reason, the demonic tenant decided to leave his "house" and go elsewhere. The man's condition improved immediately, *but the man did not invite God to come and dwell within.* In other words, the man remained neutral. What happened?

The demon returned with seven other demons worse than himself, and the man's condition was abominable.

"Neutrality in religion is always cowardice," wrote Oswald Chambers. "God turns the cowardice of a desired neutrality into terror."

Taking sides with Jesus means much more than saying the right things, like the woman who cried, "Blessed is the womb that bore You, and the breasts which nursed You" (v. 27, NKJV). She was certainly sincere, but that was not enough. *We take sides with Jesus Christ when we hear His Word and obey it* (see 6:46-49 and 8:19-21).

3. Opportunity (11:29-36)

Because He knew what was in their hearts, Jesus was not impressed by the big crowds, but the disciples were. In order to keep the Twelve from being swayed by "success," Jesus gave them some insights into what was really happening as they ministered the Word. He used three illustrations to show the seriousness of spiritual opportunities.

Jonah (vv. 29-30, 32). The leaders kept asking Jesus for a sign to prove that He was the Messiah. The only sign He promised was "the sign of Jonah the prophet," which is *death, burial, and resurrection.* It is the resurrection of our Lord that proves He is the Messiah, the Son of God (Rom. 1:4), and this is what Peter preached to Israel on the Day of Pentecost (Acts 2:22ff). The witness of the early church was centered on Christ's resurrection (Acts 1:22; 3:15; 5:30-32; 13:32-33). Jonah was a living miracle and so is our Lord Jesus Christ.

Solomon (v. 31). The emphasis here is on the wisdom of a king, not the works of a prophet. The Queen of Sheba traveled many miles to hear the wisdom of Solomon (1 Kings 10), but here was the very Son of God *in their midst,* and the Jews would not believe His words! Even if Jesus had performed a sign, it would not have changed their hearts. They needed the living wisdom of God, but they were content with their stale religious tradition.

The important thing about these illustrations is that *they involved Gentiles*. When Jonah preached to the Gentiles in Nineveh, they repented and were spared. When a Gentile queen heard Solomon's wisdom, she marveled and believed. If, with all their privileges, the Jews did not repent, then the people of Nineveh and the Queen of Sheba would bear witness against them in the last judgment. The Lord gave Israel so many opportunities, yet they would not believe (13:34-35; John 12:35-41).

The third illustration was from daily life, not from history, and was one Jesus had used before (Matt. 6:22-23). God's Word is a light that shines in this dark world (Ps. 119:105; Prov. 6:23). But it is not enough that the light be shining *externally*; it must enter our lives before it can do any good. "The entrance of Thy words giveth light; it giveth understanding unto the simple" (Ps. 119:130). The brightest sun cannot enable a blind man to see.

When we trust Jesus Christ, our eyes are opened, the light shines in, and we become children of light (John 8:12; 2 Cor. 4:3-6; Eph. 5:8-14). The important thing is that we take advantage of the light and have a *single outlook of faith*. If we keep one eye on the things of God and the other eye on the world (1 John 2:16), the light will turn into darkness! There is no "twilight living" for the Christian, for God demands total submission and obedience (v. 23).

Three men in the Bible illustrate this truth. They began in the light and ended up in the darkness because they were double-minded. The name *Samson* probably means "sunny," yet he ended up a blind slave in a dark dungeon because he yielded to the "lust of the flesh" (Jud. 16). Lot began as a pilgrim with his uncle Abraham. He ended as a drunk in a cave, committing incest (Gen. 19:30-38), because he yielded to "the lust of the eyes" (Gen. 13:10-11). Lot wanted to serve two masters and look in two directions!

King Saul began his reign as a humble leader but his pride led him to a witch's cave (1 Sam. 28), and he died of suicide on the field of battle (1 Sam. 31). His sin was "the pride of life"; he would not humble himself and obey the will of God.

Each of us is controlled either by light or darkness. The frightening thing is that some people have so hardened themselves against the Lord that *they cannot tell the difference!* They think they are following the light when, in reality, they are following the darkness. The scribes and Pharisees claimed to "see the light" as they studied the law, but they were living in the darkness (see John 12:35-50).

3. Hypocrisy (11:37-54)

At this stage in Christ's ministry, when the religious leaders were bent on destroying Him, why would a Pharisee invite Him to his home for a meal? If he had been sincerely seeking truth, he would have talked with our Lord privately. It seems obvious that he was looking for an opportunity to accuse Jesus, and he thought he had it when Jesus did not practice the ceremonial washing before eating (Mark 7:2-3). Knowing what the host was thinking, Jesus responded by giving a "spiritual analysis" of the Pharisees.

He exposed their folly (vv. 37-41). The basic error of the Pharisees was thinking that righteousness was only a matter of external actions, and they minimized internal attitudes. They were very careful to keep the outside clean, but they ignored the wickedness within. They seemed to forget that the same God who created the outside also created the inside, the "inner person" that also needs cleansing (Ps. 51:6, 10).

The Pharisees boasted of their giving (Matt. 6:1-4; Luke 18:11-12), but they did not give *what was within* to the Lord. The way to make the *outside* pure is to make the *inside* pure (v. 41). Kenneth Wuest translates this verse, "Rather, the things which are inside give as alms, and behold, all things are clean to you" (ET). The way to clean up a dirty vocabulary is not to brush your teeth but to cleanse your heart.

He denounced their sins (vv. 42-52). These six "woes" parallel the "woes" in Matthew 23. Jesus started with the sins of the Pharisees (vv. 42-44) and then turned to the sins of the scribes, for it was their interpretations of the law that formed the basis for the whole Pharisaical system (vv. 45-52).

The first three "woes" denounce the Pharisees for their *wrong priorities*. They were careful about tithing even the tiny leaves and seeds from the herbs, but they forgot about important things like justice and love (Micah 6:7-8). They majored on the minors! Jesus did not say they should stop tithing but that they should put their religious activities into proper perspective.

They also put *reputation* above *character*. They thought that sitting in the right seats and being acknowledged by the right people would make them spiritual. Reputation is what people think we are; character is what God knows we are.

The comparison in verse 44 must have infuriated the host and the other Pharisees who were present. The Jews had to be especially careful about ceremonial defilement from dead bodies (Num. 19:11-22; note especially v. 16), so they made sure the graves were carefully marked. But the Pharisees were like *unmarked graves* that did not look like graves at all! This meant that they were *unconsciously defiling others when they thought they were helping them become holier!* Instead of helping people, the Pharisees were harming them.

The scribes felt the sting of our Lord's words and tried to defend themselves. Jesus used three vivid illustrations in answering them: burdens, tombs, and keys.

The scribes were good at adding to the burdens of the people, but they had no heart for helping them carry those burdens. What a tragedy when "ministers" of God's Word create more problems for people who already have problems enough! A pastor friend of mine prays daily, "Lord, help me today not to add to anybody's problems." Jesus had these "religious burdens" in mind when He gave the gracious invitation recorded in Matthew 11:28-30.

The scribes were also good at "embalming" the past and honoring the prophets who had been martyred by the religious establishment *to which they belonged.* Both Bible history and church history reveal that true servants of God are usually rejected by the people who most need their ministry, but the next generation will come along and honor these people. The Pharisees were like "hidden graves," but the scribes built elaborate tombs!

The first recorded martyrdom in the Old Testament is that of Abel, and the last is that of Zechariah (see Gen. 4:1-15 and 2 Chron. 24:20-27, and remember that 2 Chron. is the last book in the Hebrew Bible). Jesus did not suggest that the scribes and Pharisees were *personally* responsible for killing the Old Testament prophets. Rather, He was affirming that *people just like the scribes and Pharisees* did these terrible things to God's servants. Their ultimate crime would be the crucifixion of the Son of God.

Finally, the scribes were guilty of robbing the common people of the knowledge of the Word of God. It was bad enough that they would not enter the kingdom themselves, but they were hindering others from going in! It is a serious thing to teach God's Word and not everyone is supposed to do it (James 3:1). Unfortunately, what some people call "Bible study" is too often just a group of unprepared people exchanging their ignorance.

But there is another side to this: the scribes convinced the people that nobody could understand and explain the law except the trained and authorized teachers. We have some of that arrogant attitude showing itself today. Teachers who overemphasize the Bible languages give people the impression that the Holy Spirit cannot teach anyone who does not know Greek and Hebrew. There are so many "study Bibles" these days (and many of them are helpful) that you wonder if a student can learn anything from a simple text Bible. We must not despise true Christian scholarship, but we must also keep things in balance.

Jesus Christ is the key to the Scriptures (24:44-48). When you take away that key, you cannot understand what God has written. As helpful and necessary as theological studies are, the most important requirements for Bible study are a yielded heart and an obedient will. Some of the best Bible teachers I have known in my own ministry were men and women who learned the truth of God's Word on their knees and on the battlefield of life. They were Spirit taught, not man taught.

He aroused their anger (vv. 53-54). Hypocrites do not want their sins exposed; it hurts their reputation. Instead of opposing the Lord, these men should have been bowing down before Him and seeking His mercy. They deliberately began to attack Him with "catch questions" in hopes they could trap Him in some heresy and then arrest Him. What a disgraceful way to treat the Son of God.

But there are religious systems today that are very much like the system defended by the scribes and Pharisees. The leaders interpret and apply the Word for the followers and you are not permitted to ask embarrassing questions or raise objections. The leaders exploit the people and do little or nothing to ease their burdens. Worst of all, the leaders use the system to cover up their own sins. God's truth should set us free, but these groups only lead people into more and more bondage.

God has given teachers to His church (Eph. 4:11), and we should listen to them. But we should also test what we hear by the Scriptures to make sure they are teaching the truth (1 Thes. 5:19-21), and we should not permit anyone to bring us into bondage and exploit us (2 Cor. 11:20).

It is a privilege to have the light of the Word of God and the privilege of prayer. The enemy wants to rob us of the blessings of spiritual growth and freedom. His plan is to substitute hypocrisy for reality and to encourage us to be more concerned about the outside than the inside: reputation and not character.

So serious is this danger that Jesus will have more to say about it in Luke 12. Meanwhile, let us beware!

11

Believer, Beware!

Luke 12

Our Lord's disciples may not have realized it, but they were in great danger. For one thing, they were surrounded by immense crowds of people whose major concern was not to hear spiritual truth but to see Jesus do a miracle or meet some personal need. At the same time, the scribes and Pharisees were plotting against Jesus and trying to get Him out of the way. The snare of popularity and the fear of man has brought ruin to more than one servant of God.

In chapter 12, Luke recorded five warnings from our Lord. Four of these warnings must be heeded by God's people today if we are to be faithful disciples; and the fifth warning should be heeded by a lost world.

1. Beware of Hypocrisy (12:1-12)

The word *hypocrite* comes from a Greek word that means "an actor," "one who plays a part." There are hypocrites in every walk of life, people who try to impress others in order to hide their real self. In the Christian life, a hypocrite is somebody who tries to appear more spiritual than he or she really is. These people know that they are pretending, and they hope they will not be found out. Their Christian life is only a shallow masquerade.

It is easy to see why Jesus gave this warning at this particular time. The disciples might be tempted either to gain popularity by pleasing the crowds, or avoid trouble by pleasing the scribes and Pharisees. All of us want people to like us, and it seems such an easy thing to "act the part" that others want to see.

How can we keep hypocrisy out of our lives?

First, *we must understand what hypocrisy really is* (v. 1). Jesus compared it to leaven (yeast), something that every Jew would associate with evil. (See Ex. 12:15-20. Paul also used leaven to symbolize sin. See 1 Cor. 5:6-8; Gal. 5:9.) Like yeast, hypocrisy begins very small but grows quickly and quietly. As it grows, it infects the whole person. Hypocrisy does to the ego what yeast does to bread dough: it puffs it up (see 1 Cor. 4:6, 18-19; 5:2). Soon pride takes over and the person's character deteriorates rapidly.

If we want to keep hypocrisy out of our lives, we must avoid that first bit of "leaven." Once we start to pretend, the process goes on quickly; and the longer we wait, the worse it gets. Sir Walter Scott wrote:

> O what a tangled web we weave
> When first we practice to deceive.

Jesus taught a second truth: *hypocrisy is foolish and futile* (vv. 2-3). Why? Because nothing can really be hidden. Jesus referred here primarily to His own teachings, but the principle applies to other areas of life. The Twelve might be tempted to cover or compromise the truth so that neither the crowds nor the Pharisees would be offended (see 8:16-18 and 11:33). God's truth is like light, not leaven, and it must not be hidden. The lies of the hypocrite will one day be revealed, so why go on pretending? Let your light shine!

Third, *we must understand what causes hypocrisy* (vv. 4-7). Jesus mentioned "fear" five times in these verses, so He is teaching us that a basic cause of hypocrisy is *the fear of man.* When we are afraid of what others may say about us or do to us, then we try to impress them in order to gain their approval. If necessary, we will even lie to accomplish our purposes, and this is hypocrisy. Unfortunately, many of the scribes and Pharisees were more concerned about reputation than character, what people *thought* about them than what God *knew* about them. The fear of man always brings a snare (Prov. 29:25), and Jesus wanted His disciples to avoid that snare.

The remedy for hypocrisy is to forget about what people may say and do and *fear God alone.* The fear of God is the fear that conquers all other fears, for the person who truly fears God need fear nothing else. All that men can do is kill the body, but God can condemn the soul! Since He is the final judge, and He judges for eternity, it is logical that we put the fear of God ahead of everything else. Our God knows us and cares for us. He cares for the sparrows, and we are of more value than they; so what do we have to fear from men?

But something else is involved: *we must confess Christ openly* (vv. 8-9). Once we have done this, we will have an easier time living the truth and avoiding hypocrisy. How can we fear men when we know Jesus Christ is confessing us before the Father in heaven? It is not important that men praise our names on earth, but it is important that God acknowledges us in heaven (see 2 Tim. 2:8-14).

Finally, *we must depend on the Holy Spirit* (vv. 10-12). Jesus appears to be contradicting Himself. In verses 8-9, He demands that we openly confess Him, but in verse 10, He says we can speak against Him and be forgiven. However, if we speak against the Spirit, there is no forgiveness! Does this mean that the Holy Spirit is more important than the Son of God?

Note that this statement is connected with the ministry of

the Spirit in and through the apostles (vv. 11-12). The Jewish nation rejected *God the Father* when they refused to obey John the Baptist and repent, for John was sent by the Father. They rejected *God the Son* when they asked Pilate to crucify Him. But that sin could be forgiven because there was still the ministry of the Spirit.

God did not judge the nation immediately. Instead, Jesus prayed for them as He hung on the cross (23:34; see also Acts 3:17). Then God sent the Holy Spirit who ministered through the apostles and other believers in the church. *This was the last opportunity for the nation, and they failed by rejecting the witness of the Spirit* (Acts 7:51). Luke 12:11-12 was fulfilled during the first chapters of Acts when the message went "to the Jew first" (Rom. 1:16; Acts 3:26; 13:46). Israel's third "national sin" was the stoning of Stephen (Acts 7), after which the message went out to the Samaritans (Acts 8), and then the Gentiles (Acts 10). Note that Stephen said, "You always resist the Holy Spirit" (Acts 7:51).

I do not believe that the "sin against the Holy Spirit" is committed by people today as it was by Israel centuries ago. I believe that the only "unpardonable sin" today is the final rejection of Jesus Christ (John 3:36). The Spirit of God witnesses through the Word, and it is possible for sinners to reject that witness and resist the Spirit. But the Spirit bears witness to Christ (John 16:7-15); so the way people treat the Spirit is the way they treat the Son of God.

2. Beware of Covetousness (12:13-21)

At this point, a man in the crowd interrupted Jesus and asked Him to solve a family problem. Rabbis were expected to help settle legal matters, but Jesus refused to get involved. Why? Because He knew that no answer He gave would solve the *real* problem, which was covetousness in the hearts of the two brothers. (The "you" in verse 14 is plural.) As long as both men were greedy, *no* settlement would be satisfactory. Their greatest need was to have their hearts changed. Like too many people today, they wanted Jesus to serve them but not to save them.

Covetousness is an unquenchable thirst for getting more and more of something we think we need in order to be truly satisfied. It may be a thirst for money or the things that money can buy, or even a thirst for position and power. Jesus made it clear that true life does not depend on an abundance of possessions. He did not deny that we have certain basic needs (Matt. 6:32; 1 Tim. 6:17). He only affirmed that we will not make life richer by acquiring *more* of these things.

Mark Twain once defined "civilization" as "a limitless multiplication of unnecessary necessities," and he was right. In fact, many Christians are infected with covetousness and do not know it. They think that Paul's admonition in 1 Timothy 6 applies only to the "rich and famous." Measured by the living standards of the rest of the world, most believers in America are indeed wealthy people.

Jesus told this parable to reveal the dangers that lurk in a covetous heart. As you read it, test your own responses to this farmer's various experiences.

How do you respond to the wealthy farmer's *dilemma?* Here was a man who had a problem with too much wealth! If we say, "I certainly wish I had that problem!" we may be revealing covetousness in our hearts. If suddenly you inherited a great deal of wealth, would it create a problem for you? Or would you simply praise God and ask Him what He wanted you to do with it?

There are perils to prosperity (Prov. 30:7-9). Wealth can choke the Word of God (Matt. 13:22), create snares, and temptations (1 Tim. 6:6-10, 17-19), and give you a false sense of security. People say that money does not satisfy, but it does satisfy *if you want to live on that level.* People who are satisfied only with the things that money can buy are in great danger of losing the things that money cannot buy.

This farmer saw his wealth as an opportunity to please himself. He had no thoughts of others or of God.

How do you respond to the *decisions* of the rich man? Are you saying, "Now that is shrewd business! Save and have it ready for the future!" But Jesus saw selfishness in all that this man did (note the eleven personal pronouns), and He said the man was a fool. The world's philosophy is "Take care of Number One!" But Jesus does not endorse that philosophy.

There is certainly nothing wrong with following good business principles, or even with saving for the future (1 Tim. 5:8). Jesus does not encourage waste (John 6:12). But neither does He encourage selfishness motivated by covetousness.

How do you respond to the farmer's *desires?* Are you saying, "This is the life! The man has success, satisfaction, and security! What more could he want?" But Jesus did not see this farmer enjoying life; He saw him facing death! Wealth cannot keep us alive when our time comes to die, nor can it buy back the opportunities we missed while we were thinking of ourselves and ignoring God and others.

Jesus made it clear that true life does not come from an abundance of things, nor do true success or security. This man had a false view of both life and death. He thought that life came from accumulating things, and that death was far away. On March 11, 1856, Henry David Thoreau wrote in his journal, "That man is the richest whose pleasures are cheapest." He also said, "A man is rich in proportion to the number of things which he can afford to let alone."

Finally, how do you respond to the *death* of the boastful farmer? We are prone to say, "Too bad this fellow died just when he had everything going for him! How tragic that he could not finish his great plans." But the greatest tragedy is not what the man left behind but what lay *before* him: eternity without God! The man lived without God and died without God, and his wealth was but an incident in his life. God is not impressed with our money.

What does it mean to be "rich toward God"? It means to acknowledge gratefully that everything we have comes from God, and then make an effort to use what He gives us for the good of others and the glory of God. Wealth can be *enjoyed* and *employed* at the same time if our purpose is to honor God (1 Tim. 6:10ff). To be rich toward God means spiritual enrichment, not just personal enjoyment. How tragic when people are rich in this world but poor in the next! (See Matt. 6:19-34.)

3. Beware of Worrying (12:22-34)

The rich farmer worried because he had too much, but the disciples might be tempted to worry because they did not have enough! They had given up all they had in order to follow Christ, and there were no contracts or guarantees. They were living by faith, and faith is always tested.

Worry is *destructive*. The word translated "anxious" in verse 22 means "to be torn apart," and the phrase "doubtful mind" (v. 29) means "to be held in suspense." It is the picture of a ship being tossed in a storm. Our English word *worry* comes from an old Anglo-Saxon word that means "to strangle." "Worry does not empty tomorrow of its sorrow," said Corrie Ten Boom; "it empties today of its strength."

But worry is also *deceptive*; it gives us a false view of life, of itself and of God. Worry convinces us that life is made up of what we eat and what we wear. We get so concerned about *the means* that we totally forget about *the end*, which is to glorify God (Matt. 6:33). There is a great difference between making a living and making a life.

Worry blinds us to the world around us and the way God cares for His creation. God makes the flowers beautiful, and He even feeds the unclean ravens who have no ability to sow or reap. He ought to be able to care for men *to whom He has given the ability to work.* Jesus was not suggesting that we sit around and let God feed us, for the birds themselves work hard to stay alive. Rather, He encourages us to trust Him and cooperate with Him in using the abilities and opportunities that He gives us (2 Thes. 3:6-15).

But worry even blinds us to itself. We can get to the place where we actually think that worry accomplishes good things in our lives! In verse 25, Jesus pointed out that our worries do not add one extra minute to our lives (Ps. 39:5) or one extra inch to our height. The rich farmer's fretting certainly did not lengthen his life! Instead of adding to our lives, our worries take away from our lives. People can worry themselves into the hospital or into the grave!

Once again, Jesus argued from the lesser to the greater. If God feeds the birds, He will surely feed His children. If He beautifies the plants that grow up one day and are cut down the next, surely He will clothe His own people. The problem is not His little power, for He can do anything; the problem is our little faith.

Worry is *deformative*; it keeps us from growing and it makes us like the unsaved in the world (v. 30). In short, worry is unchristian; worry is a sin. How can we witness to a lost world and encourage them to put faith in Jesus Christ if we ourselves are doubting God and worrying? Is it not inconsistent to preach faith and yet not practice it? The late chaplain of the United States Senate, Peter Marshall, once prayed "that ulcers would not become the badge of our faith." Too often they are!

How do we win over worry? The first step is to realize that *God knows our needs,* so we can trust Him to meet them. We are sheep in His little flock, children in His family, and servants in His kingdom; and He will see to it that our needs are fully met. It is His *pleasure* to give us His kingdom, so will He not give us everything that we need? (See Rom. 8:32.)

But God's pleasures and our treasures must go together. We must look at earth from heaven's point of view and make sure that we put God's kingdom first in everything. The main question is, "Where is your heart?" If our hearts are fixed on the transient things of earth, then we will always worry. But if we are fixed on the eternal, then God's peace will guard our minds and hearts (Phil. 4:6-9). We must "hang loose" when it comes to this world's goods, and be willing even to sell what we have in order to help others (Acts 2:44-45; 4:34-35). It is not wrong to own things so long as things do not own us.

4. Beware of Carelessness (12:35-53)

Jesus shifted the emphasis from being worried about the present to being watchful about the future. The themes in Luke 12 all go together, for one of the best ways to conquer hypocrisy, covetousness and worry is to look for the Lord's return. When you are "living in the future tense," it is difficult for the things of the world to ensnare you. In this section, Jesus explained how we can be ready for His return.

Waiting and watching (vv. 35-40). Jewish weddings were held at night, and a bridegroom's servants would have to wait for their master to come home with his bride. The new husband would certainly not want to be kept waiting at the door with his bride! But the servants had to be sure they were ready to go to work, with their robes tucked under their girdles so they were free to move (see 1 Peter 1:13ff).

But the remarkable thing in this story is that the master serves the servants! In Jewish weddings, the bride was treated like a queen and the groom like a king; so you would not expect the "king" to minister to his staff. Our King will minister to His faithful servants when He greets us at His return, and He will reward us for our faithfulness.

To "watch" means to be alert, to be ready, not to be caught by surprise. That is the attitude we must have toward the second coming of Jesus Christ. His coming will be like that of a thief: unannounced and unexpected (1 Thes. 5:2; Matt. 24:43; Rev. 16:15). We must be ready!

The saintly Presbyterian pastor Robert Murray McCheyne

sometimes asked people, "Do you believe that Jesus is coming today?" If they replied in the negative, he would say, "Then you had better be ready, for He is coming at an hour when you think not!"

Working (vv. 41-48). Lest we get the idea that watching and waiting are all that He requires, Jesus added this parable to encourage us to be working when He comes. The apostles had a special responsibility to feed God's household, His church; but each of us has some work to do in this world, assigned to us by the Lord. Our responsibility is to be faithful when He comes. We may not appear successful in our own eyes, or in the eyes of others; but that is not important. The thing God wants is faithfulness (1 Cor. 4:2).

Once a believer starts to think his Master is *not* coming back, his life begins to deteriorate. Our relationship with others depends on our relationship to the Lord; so if we stop looking for Him, we will stop loving His people. The motive for Christian life and service must be a desire to please the Lord and be found faithful at His return.

I do not think that verse 46 teaches that unfaithful believers lose their salvation, because our going to heaven depends on faith in Jesus Christ and not good works (Eph. 2:8-10; 2 Tim. 2:11-13). The phrase "cut him in sunder" means "cut him off, separate him"; and "unbelievers" can also be translated "unfaithful." Our Lord will separate the faithful believers from the unfaithful; He will reward the faithful, but the unfaithful servants will lose their rewards (1 Cor. 3:13-15).

God's judgment will be fair. It will be based on what the servants know of God's will. This is not to suggest that the more ignorant we are, the easier time we will have at the Judgment Seat of Christ! We are admonished to know God's will (Rom. 12:2; Col. 1:9) and to grow in our knowledge of Jesus Christ (2 Peter 3:18). Jesus is stating a general principle: the more we have from God, the greater our accountability before God.

Warring (vv. 49-53). As we wait, watch and work, we will not have an easy time, because we are aliens in enemy territory. The images Jesus used—fire, baptism, division—speak of opposition and conflict. To the Jews, fire was a symbol of judgment; and our Lord's coming into this world did bring judgment (John 9:39-41).

Our Lord's "baptism" in verse 50 refers to His suffering and death, which was pictured by His baptism in the Jordan. (See Psalm 42:7 and Jonah 2:3, and note His reference to Jonah in Luke 11:29-30.) The apostles certainly received a baptism of suffering as they witnessed for Christ after Pentecost.

Luke opened his book announcing "peace on earth" (2:14), but now he has the Lord seemingly contradicting this promise. Jesus does give peace to those who trust Him (Rom. 5:1), but often their confession of faith becomes a declaration of war among their family and friends. Jesus is a cause of division (see John 7:12, 43; 9:16; 10:19). But even if there is not "peace on earth," there is "peace in heaven" (19:38) because of the finished work of Jesus Christ on the cross.

After instructing His disciples, Jesus turned and gave a final warning to the people around Him.

5. Beware of Spiritual Dullness (12:54-59)

Jesus used two illustrations to impress on the crowds the importance of discernment and diligence in spiritual matters. First, He talked about the weather, and then He talked about a law suit.

Discernment (vv. 54-57). If people were as discerning about spiritual things as they are about the weather, they would be better off! The crowd could predict a storm, but it could not foresee the coming judgment. It knew that the temperature was about to change, but it could not interpret the "signs of the times." The Jewish nation had the prophetic Scriptures for centuries and should have known what God was doing, but their religious leaders led them astray.

How tragic that men today can predict the movements of the heavenly bodies, split atoms, and even put men on the moon; but they are blind to what God is doing in the world. They know how to get to the stars, but they do not know how to get to heaven! Our educated world possesses a great deal of scientific knowledge but not much spiritual wisdom.

Diligence (vv. 58-59). Anyone will do whatever is necessary to stay out of prison, but how many people will apply that same concern and diligence to stay out of hell? If lawyers and judges examined God's Word as diligently as they examine their law books, they will gain a wisdom that the law cannot give.

The nation of Israel was marching to judgment, and the Judge was Almighty God, yet they would not seek for terms of peace (13:34-35). Jesus knew that the Roman armies would come to destroy the city and the temple (19:41-44), but He could not convince the people to repent. Their debt was mounting up and they would pay the last mite.

We must apply these truths to our own lives personally. If we knew a storm was coming, we would prepare for it. If we knew the officer was coming to take us to court, we would get a lawyer and try to settle the case out of court. The storm of God's wrath is coming, and the judge is already standing before the door (James 5:9).

"Behold, now is the accepted time; behold, now is the day of salvation" (2 Cor. 6:2).

12

Questions and Answers

Luke 13

A Jewish student asked his teacher, "Rabbi, why is it that when I ask you a question, you always reply by asking me another question?"

The rabbi replied, "So why shouldn't I?"

As Jesus continued His journey toward Jerusalem, He encountered four situations involving questions that had to be answered. "To question a wise man is the beginning of wisdom," says a German proverb. Not everyone who questioned the Lord did so from a right motive, but that did not stop Jesus from teaching them what they needed to know. As you study His replies in Luke 13, you can learn more about Him and His ministry, and also more about living the Christian life so as to please Him.

1. A Political Question about Justice (13:1-9)

Pontius Pilate, the Roman governor, did not get along with the Jews because he was insensitive to their religious convictions. For example, he brought the official Roman ensigns into Jerusalem and infuriated the Jews who resented having Caesar's image in the Holy City. Pilate threatened to kill the protestors *and they were willing to die!* Seeing their determination, the governor relented and moved the ensigns to Caesarea, but that did not stop the hostilities.

The atrocity mentioned in verse 1 may have taken place when Pilate "appropriated" money from the temple treasury to help finance an aqueduct. A large crowd of angry Jews gathered in protest; so Pilate had soldiers *in civilian clothes* mingle with the mob. Using concealed weapons, the soldiers killed a number of innocent and unarmed Jews, and this only added to the Jews' hatred for their governor.

Since Jesus was going up to Jerusalem, anything He said about Pilate was sure to get there before Him. If He ignored the issue, the crowd would accuse Him of being pro-Roman and disloyal to His people. If He defended the Jews and accused Pilate, He would be in trouble with the Romans, and the Jewish leaders would have a good excuse to get Him arrested.

Our Lord moved the whole issue to a higher level and avoided politics completely. Instead of discussing *Pilate's* sins, He dealt with the sins of the people questioning Him. He answered their question by asking a question!

To begin with, He made it clear that human tragedies are not always divine punishments and that it is wrong for us to "play God" and pass judgment. Job's friends made this mistake when they said that Job's afflictions were evidence that he was a sinner. If we take that approach to tragedy, then we will have a hard time explaining the sufferings of the prophets and apostles, and even of our Lord Himself.

"How would you explain the deaths of the people on whom the tower in Siloam fell?" He asked. "That was not the fault of Pilate. Was it God's fault? Shall we blame Him? The eighteen who were killed were just doing their job, yet they died. They were not protesting or creating trouble."

When the blind English poet John Milton was old and obscure, he was visited one day by Charles II, son of the king that the Puritans had beheaded. "Your blindness is a judgment from God for the part you took against my father," said the king. Milton replied, "If I have lost my *sight* through God's judgment, what can you say of your father who lost his *head?*"

Jesus went on to show the logical conclusion of their argument: if God *does* punish sinners in this way, then they themselves had better repent because all men are sinners! The question is not "Why did these people die?" but "What right do you have to live?" None of us is sinless, so we had all better get prepared.

It is easier to talk about other people's deaths than it is to face our own sin and possible death. The American publishing tycoon William Randolph Hearst would not permit anyone to mention death in his presence, *yet he died.* I asked a friend of mine what the death rate was in his city, and he replied, "One apiece." Then he added, "People are dying who never died before."

According to Leviticus 19:23-25, fruit from newly planted trees was not eaten the first three years, and the fourth year the crops belonged to the Lord. A farmer would not get any figs for himself until the fifth year, but this man had now been waiting for *seven* years! No wonder he wanted to cut down the fruitless tree!

The parable has an application to individuals and to the nation of Israel. God is gracious and long-suffering toward people (2 Peter 3:9) and does more than enough to encourage us to repent and bear fruit (Matt. 3:7-10). He has had every right to cut us down, but in His mercy, He has spared us. Yet we must not presume upon the kindness and long-suffering of the Lord, for the day of judgment will finally come.

But the tree also reminds us of God's special goodness to Israel (Isa. 5:1-7; Rom. 9:1-5) and His patience with them. God waited three years during our Lord's earthly ministry, but the nation did not produce fruit. He then waited about forty years more before He allowed the Roman armies to destroy Jerusalem and the temple; and during those years, the church gave to the nation a powerful witness of the Gospel message. Finally, the tree was cut down.

It is significant that the parable was "open-ended," so that the listeners had to supply the conclusion. (The Book of Jonah is another example of this approach.) Did the tree bear fruit? Did the special care accomplish anything? Was the tree spared or cut down? We have no way to know the answers to these questions, *but we can answer as far as our own lives are concerned!* Again, the question is not "What happened to the tree?" but "What will happen to *me?*"

God is seeking fruit. He will accept no substitutes, and the time to repent is NOW. The next time you hear about a tragedy that claims many lives, ask yourself, "Am I just taking up space, or am I bearing fruit to God's glory?"

2. A Legal Question about the Sabbath (13:10-21)

Liberation (vv. 10-13). If I had been crippled for eighteen years, I wonder if I would be faithful to worship God week after week in the synagogue? Surely this woman had prayed and asked God for help, and yet she was not delivered. However, God's seeming unconcern did not cause her to become bitter or resentful. There she was in the synagogue.

Ever sensitive to the needs of others, Jesus saw the woman and called her to come forward. It may have seemed heartless to the congregation for Him to do this and expose her handicap publicly (see Matt. 12:13), but He knew what He was doing. For one thing, Satan was in the synagogue and He wanted to expose him and defeat him. But He also wanted the woman to help Him teach the people an important lesson about freedom.

Not only does Satan bow people down, but so does sin (Ps. 38:6), sorrow (Ps. 42:5), and suffering (Ps. 44:25). Jesus Christ is the only one who can set the prisoner free. He spoke the word, laid His hands on her, and she was healed and gave glory to God! That was a synagogue service the people never forgot.

Indignation (v. 14). Instead of rejoicing and giving God the glory, the ruler of the synagogue (see 8:41) became very angry. He did not have the courage to express his anger to Jesus, so he scolded the congregation! But the more you ponder his tirade, the more laughable it becomes. Suppose they *did* bring their sick to be healed, who would heal them? Did *he* have that kind of power; and, if he did, why had he not used it to help people before? What a cowardly hypocrite!

The bondage of the ruler of the synagogue was worse than that of the woman. Her bondage affected only her body, but his bondage shackled his mind and heart. He was so bound and blinded by tradition that he ended up opposing the Son of God! Elbert Hubbard called tradition "a clock that tells us what time it was." The ruler of the synagogue could not "discern this time" (vv. 12:56) and he stood condemned.

Vindication (vv. 15-17). Jesus could have healed this woman on any other day of the week. After all, she had been bound for eighteen painful years, and one more day would have made little difference. But He deliberately chose the Sabbath Day because He wanted to teach a lesson about freedom. Note the repetition of the word "loose" (vv. 12, 15-16).

First, the Lord defended the woman and rebuked the ruler of the synagogue. Jesus reminded him that he treated his animals far better than he treated this poor woman. This indictment included the people in the congregation as well. Our Lord was arguing from the lesser to the greater: if God permits people to help their thirsty animals on the Sabbath, would He not want us to care for needy people made in the image of God? Any tradition that keeps us from helping others is not from God. In fact, it is easy to use tradition as an excuse for not caring for others.

Jesus said that the woman was a "daughter of Abraham,"

referring to her spiritual condition and not her physical birth (Gal. 3:7; Luke 19:9). All the Jewish women present would have been "daughters of Abraham." Does this mean that she was a converted person *before* the Lord healed her? If so, then she is the only *believer* in the New Testament who was physically afflicted because of demonic attack. (We are not sure what Paul's "thorn in the flesh" was or exactly how Satan used it to buffet Paul. See 2 Corinthians 12.)

Perhaps it is a matter of semantics, but I prefer to speak of demonic work in believers as "demon oppression" rather than "demon possession." In fact, the Greek word is "demonized," so we need not think of "possession" in spatial terms. Certainly Satan can and does attack the bodies and minds of God's people. Some Satanic oppression could last for many years until someone detects that Satan is at work. Not all sickness is caused by demons (6:17-19), so we must not blame everything on Satan.

There were people in the congregation who hoped to use this Sabbath violation to accuse Jesus, but He left them so ashamed that they said nothing. The lesson that He taught was clear: Satan puts people into bondage, but true freedom comes from trusting Christ. The Sabbath that God wants to give us is a "heart rest" that comes through His grace and not from obeying traditions (Matt. 11:28-30).

The parables in verses 18-21 were probably spoken to the congregation just before Jesus and the Twelve departed from the synagogue. He had used these parables before and the disciples understood them (Matt. 13:31-33, 51). Some see in them a picture of the visible outward growth of the kingdom (the mustard seed) and the invisible inward influence of the kingdom (the leaven). By using these parables, Jesus was saying, "You Jewish religious leaders may hold to your dead traditions and oppose the truth, but God's living kingdom will still increase. Satan will be defeated!"

But, we must keep two other considerations in mind. First,

Jesus had already used leaven as a picture of evil (12:1), and He was not likely to contradict Himself. Second, the context of Matthew 13 indicates opposition and seeming defeat for God's kingdom, not worldwide conquest. Yes, there will be ultimate victory; but meanwhile, much of the seed sown will bear no fruit, Satan will sow counterfeits, and the net will catch all kinds of fish, good and bad. I cannot find either in church history or in contemporary reports any proof that the kingdom of God has "permeated the whole world." In view of the population increase, we are losing ground!

The Jews knew their Scriptures and recognized the images that Jesus used. Leaven represented evil (Ex. 12:14-20), and a mighty tree pictured a great world kingdom (Dan. 4:20-22; Ezek. 17:22-24; 31:3-9). A mustard seed produces a shrub, not a great tree. The kingdom would be infected with false teaching (Gal. 5:1-9), and the small seed ("little flock," 12:32) would grow into an organization that would be a home for Satan. (The birds represent the evil one, Matt. 13:19.) The professing church today fits both descriptions.

3. A Theological Question about Salvation (13:22-30)

The events recorded in John 9 and 10 fit between verses 21 and 22. Note in John 10:40-42 that Jesus then left Judea and went beyond the Jordan into Perea. The events of Luke 13:22–17:10 took place in Perea as the Lord gradually moved toward Jerusalem.

The scribes often discussed the question of how many people would be saved, and somebody asked Jesus to give His thoughts on the issue. As with the question about Pilate, Jesus immediately made the matter personal. "The question is not how many will be saved, but whether or not *you* will be saved! Get that settled first, and then we can discuss what you can do to help get others saved."

I sometimes receive "theological letters" from radio listeners who want to argue about predestination, election, and other difficult doctrines. When I reply, I usually ask them about their prayer life, their witnessing, and their work in the local church. That often ends the correspondence. Too many professed Christians want to discuss these profound doctrines, but they do not want to put them into practice by seeking to win people to Jesus Christ! D.L. Moody prayed, "Lord, save the elect, and then elect some more!"

"Many . . . will seek to enter in, and shall not be able" (v. 24). Why? The parable tells us why, and it focuses primarily on the Jewish people of that day. However, it has a personal application to all of us today.

Jesus pictured the kingdom as a great feast, with the patriarchs and prophets as honored guests (v. 28). But many of the people who were invited waited too long to respond; and, when they arrived at the banquet hall, it was too late and the door was shut (see 14:15-24; Matt. 22:1-14).

But why did they wait so long? The parable suggests several reasons. To begin with, salvation is not easy; the sinner must enter a narrow gate and walk a narrow way (v. 24; also see 9:23ff). The world's crowd is on the easy way, the way that leads to destruction (Matt. 7:13-14), and it is much easier to walk with them.

Another reason for their delay was their false sense of security. Jesus had been among them; they had even eaten with Him and enjoyed His fellowship, *yet they had never trusted Him.* God gave the nation many privileges and opportunities, but they wasted them (see 10:13-16). God is long-suffering; however, there comes a time when even God shuts the door.

Pride also played a big part: they would not humble themselves before God. In their own eyes, they were first, but in God's eyes, they were last—*and the Gentiles would come and take their place!* (See Matt. 21:43.) Imagine the "unclean Gentile dogs" sitting at the feast with Abraham, Isaac, and Jacob, while the unbelieving Jews were outside!

These people were lost because they depended on their

ancient religion to save them; but Jesus saw them as "workers of iniquity," not doers of righteousness (Isa. 64:4; Titus 1:16). It takes more than reverence for tradition to get into God's kingdom!

But the major reason was given by Jesus Himself: "Ye would not" (v. 34). Their minds had been instructed by the Word (v. 26), and their hearts had been stirred by His mighty works, but their wills were stubborn and would not submit to Him. *This is the deadly consequence of delay.* The longer sinners wait, the harder their hearts become. "Today, if you will hear His voice, do not harden your hearts" (Heb. 4:7).

The Spanish composer Manuel de Falla was notorious for not answering his mail. When he heard that a friend had died, the composer said, "What a pity! He died before I answered his letter, which he sent me five years ago!"

When sinners fail to answer *God's* invitation to His feast, *they are the ones who die.* They are "thrust out" of the joys of the kingdom and are punished with "weeping and gnashing of teeth" (v. 28). It is a picture of people who are overwhelmed with regret because they see how foolish they were to delay; but, alas, it is too late. One of the agonies of hell will be the remembrance of opportunities wasted.

What is the answer? "Strive to enter in at the narrow gate!" (v. 24) The word *strive* comes from the sports arena and describes an athlete giving his best to win the contest. Our English word *agonize* comes from this word. If people today would put as much effort into things spiritual as they do things athletic, they would be much better off.

4. A Personal Question about Danger (13:31-35)

Jesus was in Perea, which was ruled by Herod Antipas, son of Herod the Great. The Pharisees wanted to get Jesus back into Judea where the religious leaders could watch Him and ultimately trap Him, so they tried to frighten Him away.

Herod had been perplexed by our Lord's ministry and was

afraid that John the Baptist, whom he murdered, had come back from the dead (9:7-9). In fact, at one point, Herod wanted to meet Jesus so he could see Him perform a miracle! (23:8) But it appears that Herod's heart was getting harder, for now he threatened to kill Jesus. The warning the Pharisees gave (v. 31) was undoubtedly true or Jesus would not have answered as He did.

Our Lord was not afraid of danger. He followed a "divine timetable" and nothing could harm Him. He was doing the will of God according to the Father's schedule (see John 2:4; 7:30; 8:20; 13:1; 17:1). It had been decreed from eternity that the Son of God would be crucified in Jerusalem at the Passover (1 Peter 1:20; Rev. 13:8), and even Herod Antipas could not hinder the purposes of God. Quite the contrary, our Lord's enemies only helped *fulfill* the will of God (Acts 2:23; 3:13-18).

Jesus used a bit of "holy sarcasm" in His reply. He compared Herod to a fox, an animal that was not held in high esteem by the Jews (Neh. 4:3). Known for its cunning, the fox was an apt illustration of the crafty Herod. Jesus had work to do and He would accomplish it. After all, Jesus walked in the light (John 11:9-10; 9:4), and foxes went hunting in the darkness!

But Jesus also had a word to say about His nation: "It cannot be that a prophet perish out of Jerusalem" (v. 33). This parallels what He had said to the scribes and Pharisees in Luke 11:47-51. The nation not only rejected God's loving invitation to His feast, but they even killed the servants who brought them the invitation! (See Acts 13:27.)

Our Lord's heart was grieved as He saw the unbelief and rebellion around Him, and He broke out in a lamentation over the sad plight of the Jewish nation. It was a sob of anguish, not an expression of anger. His compassionate heart was broken.

The image of the hen and her chicks would be a familiar

one to an agricultural people like the Jews (see Ps. 91:4). Some of the Old Testament references to "wings" refer to the wings of the cherubim in the holy of holies in the tabernacle or temple (see Ex. 25:20; Ruth 2:12; Pss. 36:7-8; 61:4). The hen gathers her chicks when she sees danger is coming. The Pharisees told Jesus that He was in danger, when in reality *they* were in danger!

In this lament, Jesus was addressing the whole nation and not just the Pharisees who had tried to provoke Him. The people had been given many opportunities to repent and be saved, but they had refused to heed His call. "House" refers both to the "family" of Jacob ("the house of Israel") and to the temple ("the house of God"), both of which would be "left desolate." The city and temple were destroyed and the people were scattered.

But there is a future for Israel. The time will come when their Messiah will return and be recognized and received by the people. They will say, "Blessed is He that cometh in the name of the Lord" (v. 35; also see Ps. 118:26). Some of the people would use these words at His "triumphal entry" (19:38), but they will not have their fulfillment until His coming in glory (see Matt. 24:30-31; Zech. 12:10; 14:4ff).

Israel's house has been left desolate. The nation has no king or priest, no temple or sacrifice (Hosea 3:4-5). But the nation has God's promise that she has not been forsaken (Rom. 11:1ff). There can be no peace on earth until the Prince of Peace (Isa. 9:6) is seated on David's throne (Isa. 11:1ff).

Pray for the peace of Jerusalem! (Ps. 122:6)

Strive to enter in at the narrow gate!

Chapter One

Hear the Good News
(Luke 1)

1. What is Luke's emphasis in his gospel?

2. In what different ways did people respond to the Good News of the Gospel?

3. Why do you think God often speaks to His people when they are active?

4. After the angel announced the joyous news that Zechariah (Zacharias) and Elizabeth would have a son, what big mistake did Zechariah make?

5. What character traits can be seen in Mary's response to the angel's surprising visit?

6. Why was Zechariah's question "How can I be sure of this?" different from Mary's "How will this be?"

7. What expressions of joy do you read about as Mary visited Elizabeth?

8. What did God do for Mary? What did God do for others? (see Luke 1:46-55)

9. What four pictures of the Incarnation do we see in Zechariah's hymn? What do they mean?

10. What are the results of the victory of salvation? (see Luke 1:74-75)

Chapter Two

The Lord Is Come!
(Luke 2)

1. Why were Joseph and Mary careful to obey the law of the Lord and of the civil authorities? What makes their obedience different from that of the Pharisees of the day?

2. Read Matthew 5:17-18 and Galatians 4:4. Why did God choose to send the Savior to us under the Law, not above it?

3. Though as a newborn, Jesus was as weak as any other human baby, what was a major difference between Jesus and other humans as far as heaven was concerned?

4. How did God work His sovereign plan through Caesar Augustus?

5. What prophecies had been made about the Messiah?

6. Why was the first announcement of the Messiah's birth given to lowly shepherds? In what way are the shepherds good examples for us today?

7. Why is "fear not" one of the key themes of the Christmas story?

8. What was our Lord's relationship to the Law?

9. What was the "consolation of Israel" that Simeon and Anna were waiting for?

10. How is Jesus a great example for all young people?

Chapter Three

This Is the Son of God!
(Luke 3-4)

1. Who are the witnesses Luke presents to show that Jesus Christ is the Son of God? How do these witnesses affect your faith?

2. In what way was John's baptism unusual? What was his purpose and message?

3. How is the Holy Trinity shown at Jesus' baptism?

4. Why does Luke include a genealogy of Jesus?

5. Why was Jesus tempted by Satan?

6. In what ways is Jesus' response to temptation a model for us?

7. What does it mean that "there are no 'shortcuts' in the Christian life"?

8. What does it mean to tempt God?

9. Why did the Jews in the temple become antagonistic toward Jesus after His sermon on Isaiah 61:1-2?

10. In what way was Jesus proclaiming to usher in the Year of Jubilee? In what ways have you been freed or healed?

Chapter Four

The Difference Jesus Makes
(Luke 5)

1. What qualities of fishermen make for success in serving the Lord?

2. How does Peter respond to the fish miracle? (see Luke 5:8) What does that say about Peter's view of Jesus?

3. How is sin like leprosy? How was the leper changed? How can a sinner be changed?

4. Why do you think Jesus, the Son of God, needed to slip away to pray? List some times and locations that you like to be alone with God?

5. What was Jesus teaching about Himself when He said He had authority on earth to forgive sins?

6. What did the Lord's miracles demonstrate and reveal?

7. How did Matthew respond to Jesus' call of "Follow Me"? How have you responded to His call?

8. What is the first step toward healing "sin sickness"? What is the only remedy?

9. What is the meaning of the patched garment and the wine and wine skins? What is "new" that Jesus brings to us?

10. Peter, the leper, the paralytic, and Matthew were changed by encountering Jesus. In what ways were they changed? How have you been changed by your encounter with Jesus?

Chapter Five

So What's New? Everything!
(Luke 6)

1. What three new spiritual entities does Jesus establish to replace the Jewish religion?

2. What are some differences between the Sabbath and the Lord's Day?

3. What was Jesus saying when He claimed to be Lord of the Sabbath?

4. Wiersbe says "God is more concerned about meeting human needs than He is about protecting religious rules." When have you felt a conflict between needs and rules? How did you resolve it?

5. What was the purpose of the Sabbath? How had the legalists distorted it? How did Jesus show them their error?

6. Why did Jesus need to pray all night before choosing the twelve apostles?

7. How can Jesus' choice of those apostles be an encouragement to us today?

8. What do the words blessed or blessing connote?

9. What inner attitudes must we have in order to experience the blessings of the Christian life?

10. What is the difference between a person who builds on sand and one who builds on rock?

Chapter Six

Compassion in Action
(Luke 7)

1. What was so impressive about this Roman centurion in Luke 7? What did he marvel at? What was the outcome?

2. When have you seen the "divine timetable" at work in your life?

3. How did the crowd respond to the miracle of raising up the widow's dead son? How do you think you would respond if you saw a miracle like that?

4. How are doubt and unbelief different?

5. What should be the church's first priority? Where does humanitarian service and reform fit in?

6. What does it mean that the least person in the kingdom of God is greater than John?

7. Why were the sins of the sinful woman forgiven by Jesus? What did NOT save her?

8. How can a person like Simon the Pharisee miss receiving God's forgiveness?

9. From the way Jesus dealt with the needs of the centurion, the widow, John the Baptist, and the sinful woman, what guidelines or actions, however simple, can we find to use as we seek to follow in His steps?

Chapter Seven

Lessons about Faith
(Luke 8)

1. How does Wiersbe summarize Jesus' teaching about how faith comes to a person?

2. What is the object and basis of a Christian's faith? What is the proof of salvation?

3. What is the full meaning of the word hear?

4. What effect does persecution have on a Christian? On a non-Christian?

5. How could the parable of the sower encourage the disciples in their ministry? How does it encourage you?

6. How can a parable be like a picture, a mirror, and a window?

7. Why is it important that faith be tested?

8. What four challenges did Jesus overcome in this chapter? In what specific challenges do you need victory through Jesus?

9. How is the faith of demons different from saving faith?

10. What do the three recorded resurrections teach us about Jesus and about salvation?

Chapter Eight
A Many-Sided Ministry
(Luke 9)

1. Why did the disciples need Jesus' power and authority when they were sent out to minister? What is our connection to this power and authority?

2. After Jesus withdrew with the disciples, the crowds followed. How did Jesus respond to these people?

3. What can we learn from the account of the feeding of the five thousand?

4. Why is "apprentice" a particularly good synonym for "disciple"?

5. Why didn't the Twelve understand about Jesus' death and resurrection?

6. What does it mean for you to deny yourself and take up your cross daily?

7. What were the purposes of the Transfiguration? How can we have a spiritual "transfiguration" experience?

8. What were three "lacks" of His followers that Jesus grieved over?

9. How did Jesus turn what seemed like interruptions and intrusions into kingdom opportunities?

10. What is your attitude toward ministry interruptions? How can you become more open to them?

Chapter Nine

What in the World Does a Christian Do?
(Luke 10)

1. According to Wiersbe, what is the threefold ministry of every Christian believer?

2. When we see the great need or harvest, what are we to pray for? What is our personal responsibility?

3. What was the threefold joy of the seventy?

4. What is the greatest miracle of all?

5. When the lawyer asked Jesus what he could do to inherit eternal life, why did Jesus direct him to the Law?

6. Why were the actions of the Good Samaritan so shocking to the Jews?

7. Who is your neighbor? What do you need to do for your neighbor? Why does being a neighbor involve sacrifice?

8. What is the key to balancing work and worship?

9. What does "take time to be holy" mean to you? How are you doing in this area?

10. How do you keep busyness under control in your life?

Chapter Ten

Learning Life's Lessons
(Luke 11)

1. What, according to Wiersbe, is the greatest argument for the priority of prayer?

2. What does the Lord's prayer teach us about how to pray?

3. What responsibility do we have in prayer?

4. How does knowing the will of God affect our prayers?

5. In the parable on persistence, what does Jesus teach about prayer? How is God unlike the neighbor in the parable?

6. What does it mean for you to keep on asking, seeking, and knocking?

7. In spiritual warfare, what would it look like for a person to be neutral? Why is neutrality really a choice against Jesus Christ?

8. What were the three elements of Jesus' spiritual analysis of the Pharisees?

9. Which sins of the Pharisees and scribes did Jesus denounce? Of which of these are you most convicted?

10. What are the most important requirements for Bible study?

Chapter Eleven

Believer, Beware!
(Luke 12)

1. What are the four warnings in Luke 12 that must be heeded by Christ's disciples today?

2. How would you define hypocrisy? When are you most tempted to try to appear to be something you are not?

3. How can we keep hypocrisy out of our lives?

4. What is the cause of hypocrisy?

5. What are the cures for hypocrisy? Why must these three cures work together?

6. What does Wiersbe believe is the only unpardonable sin today?

7. What do you think Jesus meant by being "rich toward God"?

8. Why is worry so dangerous to a Christian?

9. How can we have victory over worry?

10. How can discernment and diligence ward off spiritual dullness?

Chapter Twelve

Questions and Answers
(Luke 13)

1. What does Jesus teach about tragedy and divine judgment in Luke 13:1-5?

2. How can we apply the parable of the fruitless tree to our lives?

3. Why do you think Jesus called the crippled woman forward in the synagogue before healing her?

4. What burdens people? How can Jesus help those who are burdened?

5. Why was the ruler of the synagogue indignant over the healing?

6. How can demons affect a Christian believer?

7. In what way is the kingdom of God like a mustard seed and like leaven?

8. Why did the invited guests wait too long to come?

9. What does Wiersbe say is the deadly consequence of delay?

10. Why didn't the Lord Jesus need to be afraid of danger and His enemies?